Work in Progress

Joyce Centenary Essays

Edited by *Richard F. Peterson, Alan M. Cohn,
and Edmund L. Epstein*

Southern Illinois University Press   Carbondale and Edwardsville

Library of Congress Cataloging in Publication Data
Main entry under title:

Work in progress.

Includes index.
    1. Joyce, James, 1882–1941—Criticism and interpreta-
tion—Addresses, essays, lectures. I. Joyce, James,
1882–1941. II. Peterson, Richard F. III. Cohn,
Alan M., 1926–   . IV. Epstein, Edmund L.
PR6019.O9Z957 1983   823'.912   82-16943
ISBN 0-8093-1094-5

PR
6019
.O9
Z957
1983

Contents

ALAN M. COHN

Introduction

The hundredth anniversary of the birth of James Joyce has shaken
loose an international avalanche of symposia, lectures, perfor-
mances, exhibitions, books, special journal issues, and so forth, in
honor of the occasion. This collection constitutes one more act of
homage to the Master from a group of Joyceans whose essays are
representative of some of the ways critics presently approach the
study of the man and his work. In these post-New Critical times,
those ways are varied indeed—the structuralist, semiotic, reader-
response, and deconstructionist currents (or, Miller, Culler, and
Fish, to Ec[h]o the words of our thirty-second president) can all be
detected here, if sometimes faintly. While not state-of-the-art sur-
veys in most cases, the offerings nevertheless reflect how present-day
critics tend to address the Joyce canon in their continuing efforts to
become his contemporaries.

Each of the first four essays is devoted to one of the major works.
Morris Beja examines *Dubliners* from the perspective of the "epiphany," a concept formulated by the young Joyce and long used as a
means of examining certain facets of his work. Richard Peterson
finds a rhythmic flow in *A Portrait* which helps us dig beneath the
book's impressionistic surface and beyond the personality of its protagonist and to see its narrative structuring more clearly. Shari and
Bernard Benstock explore *Ulysses* to discern how movement and spa-
tiality function in the Joycean narrative. Finally, Patrick McCarthy
considers the process whereby *Finnegans Wake* and its audience are
necessarily symbiotic partners.

The remaining six essays in the collection discuss various issues central to Joyce studies and range over all the works. Edmund Epstein and Fritz Senn each investigate how Joyce handles—or manipulates—language. Among other topics, Epstein shows Joyce's use of pun and prosody to achieve his effects, while Senn offers pert insights by considering the reader's task as a translational one. Looking at three decades of criticism, Margaret Church indicates where the study of the Viconian cycle and stream-of-consciousness has taken us in understanding the role of time in Joyce's fiction. Sheldon Brivic adduces a Joycean psychology from the oeuvre which offers an additional dimension to the study of the texts. Based partly on psychological readings, Suzette Henke's essay subjects the works to a feminist scrutiny which traces the growing maturity of Joyce's attitude toward women. And ending on an appropriately eschatalogical note, Father Robert Boyle examines the considerable residue of religious ethos that shows through Joyce's work.

Various as these essays are in their concerns and methodologies, they have in common that sophistication which marks the best contemporary scholarship on one of the most important and surely the most "modern" of twentieth-century authors. Yet, as sophisticated and insightful as Joyce criticism has become in the eighties, the prophecy no doubt still holds: we may be assured that his works will keep the scholars busy for at least 225 years more.

Work in Progress

Abbreviations

CP   *Collected Poems.* New York: Viking Press, 1957.

CW   *The Critical Writings of James Joyce*, ed. Ellsworth Mason and Richard Ellmann. New York: Viking Press, 1959.

D   *Dubliners*, ed. Robert Scholes in consultation with Richard Ellmann. New York: Viking Press, 1967.

E   *Exiles.* New York: Viking Press, 1951.

FW   *Finnegans Wake.* New York: Viking Press, London: Faber and Faber, 1939.

GJ   *Giacomo Joyce*, ed. Richard Ellmann. New York: Viking Press, 1968.

L   *Letters of James Joyce*, 3 vols. Vol. I, ed. Stuart Gilbert. New York: Viking Press, 1957; reissued with corrections 1966. Vols. II and III, ed. Richard Ellmann. New York: Viking Press, 1966.

P   *A Portrait of the Artist as a Young Man.* The definitive text corrected from the Dublin holograph by Chester G. Anderson and edited by Richard Ellmann. New York: Viking Press, 1964.

SH   *Stephen Hero*, ed. Theodore Spencer; new enl. ed. John J. Slocum and Herbert Cahoon. New York: New Directions, 1963.

SL   *Selected Letters of James Joyce*, ed. Richard Ellmann. New York: Viking Press, 1975.

U   *Ulysses.* New York: Random House, 1961.

MORRIS BEJA

One Good Look at Themselves: Epiphanies in *Dubliners*

During their dispute over the problems in bringing out an edition of *Dubliners*, James Joyce wrote the publisher Grant Richards that "I seriously believe that you will retard the course of civilisation in Ireland by preventing the Irish people from having one good look at themselves in my nicely polished looking-glass" (*L* I, 64). The history of literary criticism devoted to the stories in *Dubliners* has in fact stressed their revelatory nature: the revelations they provide a reader, and the revelations they record, throughout, for characters. Inevitably, those illuminations have been seen in terms of Joyce's own concept of "epiphany"; probably no other motif has so pervaded critical discussions of both the volume as a whole and its individual stories.[1]

Epiphany may be defined as "a sudden spiritual manifestation, whether from some object, scene, event, or memorable phase of the mind—the manifestation being out of proportion to the significance or strictly logical relevance of whatever produces it."[2] In *Stephen Hero* we are told that Stephen plans on "collecting many such moments together in a book of epiphanies" (*SH* 211); Joyce had had the same plan, although he never saw it through to completion. Of the many manuscript epiphanies which he composed, forty have survived and been published.[3] Twenty-five of them eventually found their way into Joyce's novels, none of the surviving ones into *Dubliners*; yet the connection between those manuscripts and the short stories seems especially intimate. Even the form of a story may remind one of the format of many of the manuscripts, most of which make frequent use of ellipses, and a number of which end with them. For example there is one manuscript epiphany recording a conversation about a priest:

> [Dublin: in the Stag's Head,
> Dame Lane]
> O'Mahony—Haven't you that little priest that writes poetry over there—
> Fr Russell?
> Joyce—O, yes . . . I hear he has written verses.
> O'Mahony—(*smiling adroitly*) . . . Verses, yes . . . that's the proper name
> for them. . . .[4]

The first story in *Dubliners*, "The Sisters," presents a very different conversation about a priest, but there too the fragmentary nature of the separate moment of manifestation for the boy who is listening is accentuated by the liberal use of ellipses, as the story even seems to end in the middle of a sentence:

> She stopped suddenly as if to listen. I too listened; but there was no sound in the house: and I knew that the old priest was lying still in his coffin as we had seen him, solemn and truculent in death, an idle chalice on his breast.
> Eliza resumed:
> —Wide-awake and laughing-like to himself. . . . So then, of course, when they saw that, that made them think that there was something gone wrong with him. . . . (*D* 18)

The eponymous epiphany within *Stephen Hero* is the one provided to Stephen as he walks the streets of Dublin and overhears

> . . . the following fragment of colloquy out of which he received an impression keen enough to afflict his sensitiveness very severely.
> The Young Lady—(drawling discreetly) . . . O, yes . . . I was . . . at the . . . cha . . . pel . . .
> The Young Gentleman—(inaudibly) . . . I . . . (again inaudibly) . . . I . . .
> The Young Lady—(softly) . . . O . . . but you're . . . ve . . . ry . . . wick . . . ed. . . . (*SH* 211)

We may compare that to the following fragmentary colloquy—between a young lady and two young gentlemen—from "Araby,"

which somehow leads the boy who overhears it to come to see himself "as a creature driven and derided by vanity":

At the door of the stall a young lady was talking and laughing with two
young gentlemen. I remarked their English accents and listened vaguely to
their conversation.
—O, I never said such a thing!
—O, but you did!
—O, but I didn't!
—Didn't she say that?
—Yes. I heard her.
—O, there's a . . . fib! (*D* 35)

In the end, of course, it is not so much format as the sense of illumination that reminds us of the concept of epiphany: the appearance in
so many of the stories of those separate moments of perception or
self-awareness on the part of a character, or of those fragments in
which the reader may feel suddenly illumined about an aspect of a
character's personality, or situation—or entire life.

The connection can be exaggerated: *Dubliners* after all is not to be
equated with the collection of epiphanies that never appeared, although such an identification has become a commonplace in criticism and scholarship.[5] Even the shortest of the stories cannot so defy
the realities of spatial form that it can be regarded as "sudden" in its
entirety—as "an" epiphany. Such loose terminology, and a tendency
upon the part of some critics to find epiphanies everywhere (to such
an extent that one wonders what in Joyce is *not* an epiphany), have
led a few critics to doubt the whole validity of the literary term itself
and its value in Joyce studies.[6] But its importance has persisted,
and it has been related to the most prominent of the themes and
patterns of imagery in the volume. Let me provide two examples:
the theme of bondage coupled with that of the need to escape, and
the imagery of eyes and sight.

The volume opens with the words, "There was no hope . . ."; it
ends with "the descent of their last end, upon all the living and the
dead." It is no wonder that so many of the characters we encounter
seek refuge or escape from such a world. Moreover, the first story

begins a pattern that will recur in a large number of the stories, as we realize that the frustrations and fears, as well as the hopes, associated with bondage and escape are often connected to a parental figure—in "The Sisters," the paternal figure of the dead priest. The narrator tells us that as a boy he was confused "at discovering in myself a sensation of freedom as if I had been freed from something" by the priest's death (D 12). And like other characters to come in the book, he dreams that he is "very far away, in some land where the customs were strange—in Persia, I thought" (D 13–14); but in fact it is the priest alone who has "gone to a better world" (D 15). Even in death, the priest has "taught me a great deal" (D 13).

The paternal figure in "An Encounter" is much more clearly a threat, of course; the irony is that he is encountered during an attempt to find release from the dull life the narrator has been leading, an attempt which is a result of his "hunger" for "wild sensations" and "escape": "but real adventures, I reflected, do not happen to people who remain at home: they must be sought abroad" (D 21). Real adventures also entail dangers, and the pederastic stranger is more than the boy can deal with at his age—or comprehend, despite his realization that the stranger "seemed to plead with me that I should understand him" (D 27). Yet the experience is not without result: if the boy is not yet able fully to recognize or admit the significance of the stranger, he can respond as never before to his friend Mahony, who is after all coming as if to liberate him: "And I was penitent; for in my heart I had always despised him a little" (D 28). Throughout many of the stories, a central question entails how much the possibility of a given character's rescue may be enhanced by the awareness provided by an epiphany of one's self and one's situation.

Eveline, for one, does not achieve freedom as a result of her new insight; in bondage to an occasionally violent father—the first but not the last violent paternal figure in the volume—she recognizes what she must do "in a sudden impulse of terror. Escape! She must escape!" (D 40). But she finds it impossible to do so, despite her awareness. Mr. Duffy's illumination, in "A Painful Case," comes too late for him to act upon it. Others, too, resist awareness or action or both: in "After the Race," Jimmy Doyle "knew that he would regret in the morning but at present he was glad of the rest, glad of the dark stupor that would cover up his folly" (*D* 48).

In "Counterparts," any sympathy we may feel for the entrapped Farrington because of his relationship with Mr. Alleyne is swept away as, returning to his home, he becomes himself the father-ogre; with Farrington experiencing no self-knowledge, the revelation from the fragmented slice of brutal life must be ours:

The little boy looked about him wildly but, seeing no way of escape, fell upon his knees. . . .

—O, pa! he cried. Don't beat me, pa! And I'll . . . I'll say a *Hail Mary* for you. . . . I'll say a *Hail Mary* for you, pa, if you don't beat me. . . . I'll say a *Hail Mary*. . . . (*D* 98)

Bob Doran's "instinct," in "The Boarding House," urges him "to remain free, not to marry. Once you are married you are done for, it said"—but he is oppressed by his knowledge that his bondage is inevitable in Dublin, which "is such a small city" (*D* 66), and by the overpowering Mrs. Mooney. Another ominous maternal figure is Mrs. Kearney of "A Mother," and perhaps still another is the protective Mrs. Chandler of "A Little Cloud," in which Little Chandler comes to the realization (accurate if only because he believes it to be so) that he is "a prisoner for life" (*D* 84).

In many important ways, "The Dead" stands apart from the rest of *Dubliners*, but it does share the sense of bondage and of the desirability of escape: Gabriel, like Gretta explicitly and others in the volume implicitly, hears the call of "distant music." In his after-dinner speech, Gabriel asserts that "we have all of us living duties and living affections which claim, and rightly claim, our strenuous endeavours" (*D* 204). But he has already revealed in an outburst to Miss Ivors that "I'm sick of my own country, sick of it!" (*D* 189), just as he has enviously reflected on "how cool it must be outside! How pleasant it would be to walk out alone, first along by the river and then through the park! The snow would be lying on the branches of the trees and forming a bright cap on the top of the

Wellington Monument. How much more pleasant it would be there than at the supper-table!" (*D* 192). But his fate comes at least for a time to seem more like that of the horse named Johnny—"the tragic part about Johnny" being his inability to do anything but go around in circles (*D* 207).

Gabriel, we are told, has "restless eyes" (*D* 178); again and again, the role of epiphany—and illumination, vision—and the theme of escape are connected within this volume through imagery of eyes and sight. It is striking how many of the stories are climaxed by an ending which refers significantly to eyes or the act of seeing. The narrator of "An Encounter" recognizes his new feelings for Mahony as the other boy *sees* him. In contrast, Frank cannot make contact with Eveline, whose "eyes gave him no sign of love or farewell or recognition" (*D* 41). The narrator of "Araby" tells us that "I saw myself as a creature driven and derided by vanity; and my eyes burned with anguish and anger" (*D* 35). At the end of "After the Race," the morning which Jimmy dreads comes as "the cabin door opened and he saw the Hungarian standing in a shaft of grey light" (*D* 48). "Two Gallants" closes as Corley opens his palm "slowly to the gaze of his disciple" (*D* 60). Waiting for word from her mother, Polly Mooney's "hopes and visions were so intricate that she no longer saw the white pillows on which her gaze was fixed or remembered that she was waiting for anything" (*D* 68). After recognizing his imprisonment, and then angrily shouting at his baby son, Little Chandler is confronted by his wife, and he "sustained for one moment the gaze of her eyes and his heart closed together as he met the hatred in them"—and then "tears of remorse started to his eyes" (*D* 85). Farrington's son, treated even more brutally, "looked about him wildly but, seeing no way of escape, fell upon his knees" (*D* 98). At the end of "Clay," Joe's "eyes filled up so much with tears that he could not find what he was looking for and in the end he had to ask his wife to tell him where the corkscrew was" (*D* 106). Finally, in "The Dead," Gabriel thinks of how his wife has "locked in her heart for so many years that image of her lover's eyes," and then we are told that "generous tears filled Gabriel's eyes" (*D* 223).

At the end of "The Dead," Gabriel achieves epiphany; other characters in *Dubliners* stories come to similar revelations as well (the narrator of "An Encounter" and the narrator of "Araby," for example, or Little Chandler in "A Little Cloud," or notably Mr. Duffy in "A Painful Case"—or even Eveline, before she represses all awareness). At other times no less a sensation of epiphany is conveyed, but the revelation seems totally reserved for the reader (as in "Two Gallants," or "Counterparts," or "Clay," or "Ivy Day in the Committee Room," for example). We cannot know more than Gabriel does about Gretta's past life and about her feelings for Michael Furey, for we hear from her only what he does. But if we share his ignorance and uncertainty, a compensation may be that we can also share his insight: if Gabriel achieves epiphany, we may too. Yet it is no mere accident of fate, one is tempted to assume, that the earliest surviving piece of Joyce's writing is an adolescent student essay entitled "Trust Not Appearances" (*CW* 15–16), and in *Dubliners* at least as much as in any other of his works a key question entails the reader's ultimate sense of the accuracy, validity, or completeness of a given character's illumination. Most readers will have at least some reservations: surely most of us will be less harsh on the boy at the end of "Araby" than he is on himself; while when Little Chandler at the end of "A Little Cloud" feels that he is "a prisoner for life," we may well agree—but we may not at all sense in his emotions and thoughts a genuine recognition of the major sources of that imprisonment. Even when we tend to accept a character's new awareness of his or her situation, we cannot be sure that we and the character are correct— or that the new awareness is any less fleeting than the sensation of epiphany itself. Constantly in *Dubliners* we see characters come to feel that their past understanding has been limited, or distorted, or downright wrong—so why should we doubt that they may eventually come to see their new sudden spiritual manifestations as false or even perverse? The narrator of "An Encounter" may go back to his contempt for Mahony, but even so, would we not trust—in this instance, anyway—his revelation of his shared humanity rather than any subsequent doubts about it?

In one sense, the question I am raising is irrelevant, or an imposition, if we believe that what matters is what a given character *feels* about an epiphany or the revelation it provides. An epiphany need not, after all, be "objectively" accurate; as I have argued elsewhere,[7] an epiphany is in its very conception and description a *subjective* phenomenon. So whether Mr. Duffy and the boy at the end of "Araby" are "correct" is much less relevant than how *they* feel about what they have learned. Yet while that is true, it is not the whole story either, and it is the rare reader who will exert such complete self-control as to refrain from all speculation in regard to such matters; and, I strongly believe, it is the misguided literary critic who will regard it as theoretically indefensible for a reader to be undisciplined. Most readers in the real world will almost inevitably *want* to know (whether they can or not) how legitimate it is to share in the boys' views of themselves at the end of "An Encounter" and "Araby," or in Gabriel's self-contempt in the hotel in "The Dead." We cannot know, finally; but it is striking and worth noting how cogent the epiphanies seem to be at the close of several of the stories, even as they entail illuminations about the entire lives of certain characters; we may have doubts about many of Mr. Duffy's perceptions, yet we surely agree that he has "been outcast from life's feast" (D 117). Even poor Little Chandler's revelation of imprisonment and of remorse, restricted though it is by his severely limited abilities at genuine self-perception, probably brings him to a fuller and more accurate vision of his life than the sense of his existence he has had earlier that evening.

A series of unanswered questions appears throughout the volume. As the boy in "The Sisters" reflects on the priest's "intricate questions" about the "complex and mysterious . . . institutions of the Church," he finds that he can "make no answer" (D 13). When Mangan's sister speaks to the boy in "Araby" for the first time, he does "not know what to answer" (D 31), and in his distraction he answers "few questions in class" (D 32). When Miss Ivors asks Gabriel why he is sick of his own country, he does not reply—"Of course, you've no answer," Miss Ivors observes (D 190); and later, when he asks Gretta what she is thinking about, she does "not answer nor yield wholly to his arm" and she does "not answer at once" (D 218). When an answer finally does come to a question, the effect is terrifying:

> —And what did he die of so young, Gretta? Consumption, was it?
> —I think he died for me, she answered.
> A vague terror seized Gabriel at this answer as if, at that hour when he had hoped to triumph, some impalpable and vindictive being was coming against him, gathering forces against him in its vague world. (D 220)

Thus begins a series of sudden, revelatory answers for Gabriel. All of our questions about the reliability of characters' epiphanies arise with special insistence in regard to Gabriel's in "The Dead." Some of the answers intruding themselves upon his consciousness are to questions Gabriel has never dared ask before, or thought to ask. Their cumulative effect seems to him cosmically significant; we may wonder whether they are as world-shaking as he makes them out to be, but for him they seem so—and, consequently, so they are, for him. Fittingly, they all occur on Twelfth Night, the Feast of Epiphany.

The choice of date is no doubt in part ironic, and as is frequently the case in Joyce's presentation of epiphanies, there is much irony in Gabriel's final revelations. Some of the irony appears, in retrospect, in the preparations for the epiphanies—as when we recall Gabriel's reference to Aunt Julia's singing as "a surprise and a revelation to us all to-night" (D 204) and realize that it has been Bartell D'Arcy's singing of "The Lass of Aughrim" that has in fact yielded "a surprise and a revelation." Moreover, between that song and the revelation will come additional ironic contexts, as Gabriel expects that he and Gretta will make passionate love. He longs "to be master of her strange mood," to "crush her body against his, to overmaster her" (D 217). One of the things he then discovers is the degree to which he is not truly her master—and, especially right now, not the "master of her strange mood," for she has, he comes to realize or believe, "locked in her heart for so many years that image of her lover's eyes when he had told her that he did not wish to live" (D 223). When

Gabriel recognizes that while he has been fantasizing about their love-making, Gretta has not been thinking of him at all, we may ironically recall his urging of the other dinner guests to "forget my existence, ladies and gentlemen" (D 198).

With the recollection by Gretta Conroy of Michael Furey's existence, we see—as nowhere else in the story or the entire volume—the influence of the dead upon the living. Ostensibly, what Gabriel has learned is merely that his wife once had a sweetheart about whom he has not heard. Nevertheless, he somehow experiences a sudden illumination of the entire futility of his life and self—or a series of such sudden illuminations, as when a brief glance of himself in the mirror leads a few moments later to "a shameful consciousness of his own person": "He saw himself as a ludicrous figure, acting as a pennyboy for his aunts, a nervous well-meaning sentimentalist, orating to vulgarians and idealising his own clownish lusts, the pitiable fatuous fellow he had caught a glimpse of in the mirror" (D 219–20). In its harshness and our uncertainty about its justice, Gabriel's epiphany is distinctly reminiscent of the one experienced by the boy at the end of "Araby" when he sees himself as a "creature driven and derided by vanity" (D 35). Insofar as Gabriel comes to feel that he has not lived, his revelation is even more like the one provided to Mr. Duffy at the end of "A Painful Case," or to John Marcher at the climax of Henry James's "The Beast in the Jungle." Gabriel realizes that ". . . she had had that romance in her life: a man had died for her sake. It hardly pained him now to think how poor a part he, her husband, had played in her life" (D 222). Like Marcher, although without any hint that in his case he will soon die, Gabriel comes to a sense of the inevitability of death, and he feels strangely close to the young man who died years before:

Generous tears filled Gabriel's eyes. He had never felt like that himself towards any woman but he knew that such a feeling must be love. The tears gathered more thickly in his eyes and in the partial darkness he imagined he saw the form of a young man standing under a dripping tree. Other forms were near. His soul had approached that region where dwell the vast hosts of the dead. (D 223)

Earlier, Gabriel "ironically" asks, "What was he?" Here, too, Gretta's answer is devastating in its effect upon him as she matter-of-factly replies, "He was in the gasworks." Gabriel feels "humiliated by the failure of his irony and by the evocation of this figure from the dead, a boy in the gasworks" (*D* 219).

At the end of "An Encounter," the protagonist feels "penitent" about Mahony, "for in my heart I had always despised him a little" (*D* 28). Such a sensation reflects genuine moral progress. Similarly, although there has long been a controversy about the nature and full reliability of Gabriel's epiphanies at the end of "The Dead," we may take as a sign of growth, maturation, and a new perception about himself and others, his realization of his identity with the "boy in the gasworks."

Gabriel Conroy and several characters within the volume, then, have had in the end that "one good look at themselves." So have "the Irish people." And so, for that matter, have untold numbers, throughout the world, of Joyce's readers.

Notes

1. Among those critics who have importantly or centrally associated the chief methods and approaches of *Dubliners* with epiphany are: Harry Levin, *James Joyce: A Critical Introduction*, rev. ed. (Norfolk, Conn.: New Directions, 1960); Irene Hendry [Chayes], "Joyce's Epiphanies," in *James Joyce: Two Decades of Criticism*, ed. Seon Givens (New York: Vanguard, 1963), pp. 27–46; Hugh Kenner, *Dublin's Joyce* (Bloomington: Indiana Univ. Pr., 1956); William T. Noon, S.J., *Joyce and Aquinas*, Yale Studies in English, No. 133 (New Haven, Conn.: Yale Univ. Pr., 1957); Julian Kaye, "The Wings of Daedalus: Two Stories in *Dubliners*," *Modern Fiction Studies*, 4 (1958), 31–41; William York Tindall, *A Reader's Guide to James Joyce* (New York: Noonday Pr., 1959); S. L. Goldberg, *The Classical Temper: A Study of James Joyce's Ulysses* (New York: Barnes and Noble, 1961); Florence L. Walzl, "The Liturgy of the Epiphany Season and the Epiphanies of Joyce," *PMLA*, 80 (1965), 436–50; Warren Beck, *Joyce's Dubliners: Substance, Vision, and Art* (Durham, N.C.: Duke Univ. Pr., 1969); Stanley L. Jedynak, "Epiphany as Structure in *Dubliners*," *Greyfriar*, 12 (1971), 29–56; Homer Obed Brown, *James Joyce's Early Fiction: The Biography of a Form* (Cleveland: The Press of Case Western Reserve Univ., 1972); Hélène Cixous, *The Exile of James Joyce*, trans. Sally A. J. Purcell (New

York: David Lewis, 1972); C. H. Peake, *James Joyce: The Citizen and the Artist* (London: Edward Arnold, 1977); James H. Maddox, Jr., *Joyce's Ulysses and the Assault upon Character* (New Brunswick, N.J.: Rutgers Univ. Pr., 1978).

2. Morris Beja, *Epiphany in the Modern Novel* (Seattle: Univ. of Washington Pr., 1971), p. 18. The definition is an expansion upon the one in Joyce's *Stephen Hero*, ed. Theodore Spencer, rev. John J. Slocum and Herbert Cahoon (Norfolk, Conn.: New Directions, 1963), p. 211.

3. See *The Workshop of Daedalus: James Joyce and the Raw Materials for* A Portrait of the Artist as a Young Man, ed. Robert Scholes and Richard M. Kain (Evanston, Ill.: Northwestern Univ. Pr., 1965), pp. 11–51.

4. *Workshop of Daedalus*, p. 20.

5. The habit began early, in the first two critical discussions of epiphany: in Harry Levin's *James Joyce: A Critical Introduction*, which appeared in 1941, even before *Stephen Hero* ("Such a collection has come down to us by way of *Dubliners*," p. 29) and in Theodore Spencer's Introduction to *Stephen Hero* ("*Dubliners*, we may say, is a series of epiphanies," pp. 16–17).

6. One of the most interesting of the debates about the term arose as the aftermath of an essay by Florence L. Walzl on *Dubliners* and its possible use of the liturgy of the epiphany season. Robert Scholes objected that the term "epiphany" should apply only to Joyce's manuscripts, to which Walzl replied that "Joyce himself set the pattern for the use of the term *epiphany* as a spiritual or intellectual apprehension which represented an enlightenment." See Florence L. Walzl, "The Liturgy of the Epiphany Season," and Robert Scholes and Florence L. Walzl, "The Epiphanies of Joyce," *PMLA*, 82 (1967), 152–54. Cf. Beja, *Epiphany in the Modern Novel*, pp. 84–85.

7. *Epiphany in the Modern Novel*, e.g., pp. 77–79.

2

RICHARD F. PETERSON

Stephen and the Narrative of A *Portrait of the Artist as a Young Man*

The key to the criticism of A *Portrait of the Artist as a Young Man* has been the personality of Stephen Dedalus and Joyce's own attitude or distance from that personality.[1] While the title clearly claims a special genius for Stephen—that of the artist—and modifies that genius by fixing it at a stage of potential or development—as a young man—critics have often chosen between "the artist" or "the young man" in their judgment of Joyce's intention in the novel.

Those who read the novel as a portrait of artistic genius usually sympathize with Stephen's ordeals, approve his aesthetic theory as Joyce's own, and see him triumphing over his treacherous environment by flying into a self-imposed exile to write a masterpiece.[2] Others, influenced by Hugh Kenner, find only a young man in the novel and condemn Stephen's actions, mock his aesthetics as juvenile, and judge him as a case of arrested development in spite of Stephen's talk about creating the uncreated conscience of his race. Kenner has been especially vigilant and aggressive in deprecating Stephen, describing him as a fake artist, "indigestibly Byronic," and most recently as the spiritual brother of the broken or resigned failures in *Dubliners*.[3]

This debate over Stephen's personality and whether or not he will ever write the works of genius of his creator has obviously influenced the study of the narrative form of A *Portrait*. Stephen sympathizers plunge into an impressionistic flux and see that flux forming itself into a process of becoming out of which Stephen finally emerges as the artist-creator of his own life. Stephen haters remain aloof from the narrative itself and find the novel an ironic demonstration of the failure of talent or genius to express itself except in "rebellious bohemianism."[4] They judge Stephen a hopeless product of his environment, his generation, and his own sensibility.

While the debate continues between critics who argue for an impressionistic narrative of becoming and those who see an ironic narrative demonstrating a finished state, some have perceived a double vision forming the narrative. This view takes into account what appears to be both artistic involvement and detachment within the novel. Unfortunately, since the emphasis here is on vision, or how Joyce perceives his own novel, those who see both Joycean compassion and irony have trouble deciding whether Joyce's portrait is one of compassionate irony or ironic compassion. In other words, that same enigma, the virtues and vices of Stephen's personality, also haunts those who see someone to admire and to dislike, but cannot decide where to place the emphasis.

What Stephen sympathizers, haters, and undecideds have in common is the willingness to place their attitude toward the novel's central character before their approach to the novel. While this strategy seems perfectly justifiable considering the novel's impressionistic style (some argue for a stream of consciousness), the narrative itself offers a few surprises. As Stephen advances impressionistically through the stages of crisis or development Richard Ellmann compares to "the gestation of a soul,"[5] the narrative advances within its own rhythm. In other words, Stephen's eventual discovery of his soul and his desire, whether ever realized or not, to express his discovery through the artist's imagination give a definite form to the chapters of *A Portrait*; but the narrative itself reveals a deliberate pattern of reality external to Stephen's thoughts and actions that is both visible and audible within the narrative itself.

After *A Portrait* opens with "once upon a time" (*P* 7), the time-honored incantation of the story-teller, and a brief series of sharp impressions from Stephen's early life, the narrative of the first chapter focuses on the first crisis in the development of the artist.

Through three episodes of Stephen's childhood, we see Stephen's early, confused attempts to find his proper place in the universe. All three events—his illness after being shoved by Wells into the square ditch, the violent political quarrel at the Christmas dinner table, and the pandying from Father Dolan—disrupt the proper order of things. Stephen's confusion is actually physical in the Clongowes episodes because his vision is distorted first by the "collywobbles" and then by the accidental breaking of his glasses. Only when Stephen tells the rector about the "unjust and cruel and unfair" (P 53) pandying and is assured that the rector will speak to Father Dolan is the focus of authority restored in Stephen's mind, even though the experiences, disruptive in themselves, now form a pattern that will lead Stephen to his fateful decision to reject the priesthood of the Roman Catholic Church and become a priest of art.

While Stephen's experiences in the first chapter appear to leap forward fitfully because of the impressionistic style and structure of *A Portrait*, there is a definite and separate pattern to the episodes that give the chapter a good measure of its unity and balance. Though there is a gap of several months between each major experience in Stephen's life, we have the chance to observe a season-by-season movement from episode to episode. The first impression of Stephen's life at Clongowes is cloaked in the dampness and gloom of the early October days of 1891. Stephen, "caught in the whirl of a scrimmage" (P 9) of footballers, anticipates changing the number pasted up inside his desk from seventy-seven to seventy-six (the days remaining before the holiday), and dreams of Parnell's body being returned to Dublin.[6] In the second episode, the narrative advances to Christmas as the scene shifts to Stephen's first Christmas Day dinner at his father's table. The holiday anticipated at Clongowes is now clearly identified and the reason for the vividness of Parnell's death in Stephen's mind is underscored by the content of the quarrel at the dinner table. In the final episode, the second at Clongowes, the seasonal pattern of the chapter is definitely established. While Stephen shares in the atmosphere of fear, he notices that "there was no play on the football grounds for cricket was coming" (P 41). Shortly after the pandying, he finds that he "could not eat the blackish fish fritters they got on Wednesdays in Lent" (*P* 53), and after his visit to the rector, he sees that the "fellows were practising long shies and bowing lobs and slow twisters" (*P* 59). Thus, while Stephen undergoes three experiences that momentarily bewilder his sense of the proper order of things and form an early chain of events that will lead to his decision to become the artist, the world around him asserts its separate reality as the seasons advance from fall to winter to spring. As Stephen moves toward the moment when he discovers his soul and the nature in which he will express his discovery, the early narrative pattern of *A Portrait* gives to the impending moment an air of inevitability.

Before Stephen discovers his soul, however, he learns through another fitful series of disturbing and painful impressions that he has a body. The advancing tide of Stephen's puberty and the winding journey in the second chapter from Mercedes to E—— C—— and finally to the prostitute is also apprehended within a definite movement of the seasons. Even though several years have elapsed since Stephen's crisis of authority, the seasons hold to their own pattern as Stephen now feels the first stirrings of sexuality. As Stephen endured the humiliation of the pandying in the early spring, so he now pores over his ragged translation of *The Count of Monte Cristo* and becomes a leader of a gang of adventurous youths during "the first part of the summer" (*P* 60). The "coming of September" (*P* 63) fails to trouble him this year because he is not being sent to Clongowes. Shortly after, the Dedalus family moves to the city of Dublin, Stephen observes the "jovial array of shops lit up and adorned for Christmas" (*P* 67), and attends a party at Harold's Cross. When he learns that his father has made arrangements for him at Belvedere the season appears to be turning once again.

The next time we see Stephen he is now firmly set in the pattern of Belvedere life. The Whitsuntide play in which he has the chief role of the farcical pedagogue takes place during his second year at the Jesuit day school. There is another leap in the narrative, this time nearly two years, but the seasons still pass in their natural order.

While Stephen talks to Heron and his friend just before the beginning of the play, he remembers "a raw spring morning" (*P* 79) toward the end of his first term at Belvedere when he was accused of heresy in his essay, and, a few nights later, was abused by Heron and two other youths after he defended Byron as a better poet than Tennyson. This memory clearly establishes the season when Stephen learns from his father that he is being sent to Belvedere,[7] and places that scene within a deliberate narrative pattern that has advanced in the present episode to late spring since Whitsuntide week begins on the seventh Sunday after Easter.

When Stephen visits Cork with his father, he is conscious of the summer atmosphere of the "warm sunny city" (*P* 88) and the whispering leaves of the blooming trees that speak to the fever in his blood. In the next episode, the seasons advance again as a "keen October wind" (*P* 97) cuts through the figure of Stephen's thinly clad mother on the family's way from the bank of Ireland with the exhibition and essay prize money. When an artificial and all too "swift season of merrymaking" (*P* 97) fails to stay the relentless decline of the family's fortune or the brutal urgings of his body, Stephen prowls the streets during the "veiled autumnal evenings" (*P* 99) until he finally surrenders in a swoon into the arms of a prostitute.

By the end of the second chapter, Stephen has experienced two major crises and his life has advanced several years in the process. While Stephen's early ordeals have been presented through a series of rapidly moving, almost fitful impressions, the narrative has carefully recorded the passing of the seasons. In the last three chapters of *A Portrait*, the impressions of Stephen's life do not move as rapidly within the context of each chapter or from chapter to chapter because of the approaching moment of discovery and decision in his life, but the narrative still gives the world around Stephen its own separate reality.

Two other patterns have also emerged by the end of the second chapter to reinforce the idea of external reality in *A Portrait*. While the seasons have passed in their inexorable order, we have also had the chance to hear and feel time moving along its inevitable course, even though clocks never actually tick in the early chapters. At the end of the first chapter, Stephen experiences the first thrill of being alone and free, but when the cheers of the students die away, he hears "through the quiet air the sound of the cricket bats: pick, pack, pock, puck: like drops of water in a fountain falling softly in the brimming bowl" (*P* 59). In the second chapter, the association of time and water becomes more pronounced. As Stephen struggles with his growing sexuality, he feels his heart dancing like "a cork upon a tide" (*P* 69). And when he finally admits his failure "to build a breakwater of order and elegance against the sordid tide of life without him," he also recognizes that he is incapable of damming "the powerful recurrence of the tides within him" (*P* 98).

While time and the body's rhythm, associated with the movement of the tides, advance ineluctably through the early chapters, another pattern, reflective of the human desire to give a special order and religious meaning to experience, emerges in *A Portrait*. In each of the first two chapters, a feast day of the Church is the focal point of Stephen's crisis. The violent political quarrel takes place at Christmas, a day invested not only with great religious meaning but one that has taken on a special significance for Stephen because it represents his first school holiday and his first Christmas dinner with his mother and father. In the second chapter, Stephen endures his greatest frustration and remembers his worst humiliation on the evening of the Whitsuntide play. While the play itself has a Pentecostal effect upon Stephen, briefly returning him to the innocent mirth of boyhood, his painful memory of the beating and his frustrated anticipation of meeting the girl of his secret desires jar his nerves and increase the riot in his blood to the point that only the rank odor of horse piss and rotted straw can calm him—for the moment.

At the beginning of the third chapter, the seasons appear about to continue their separate and inevitable pace. The "veiled autumnal evenings" that found Stephen prowling through nighttown have now advanced to the days followed by the "swift December dusk" (*P* 102). There are, however, no great chronological leaps within the chapter. Instead, the narrative is limited to the few days of Stephen's spiritual trial. Stephen discovers the mortal dangers to his soul during the retreat in honor of Saint Francis Xavier's feast day, which is celebrated on the third day in December. Most of the chapter takes place from Wednesday, when Father Arnall begins his fiery sermon, to Saturday, the feast day of Saint Francis, when Stephen receives holy communion and believes that he has overcome the urgings of his body by returning in spirit to the innocence of boyhood: "Another life! A life of grace and virtue and happiness! It was true. It was not a dream from which he would wake. The past was past" (*P* 146).

In the third chapter, then, while Stephen is undergoing that "slow and dark birth" (*P* 203) of the soul he describes in a later scene with Lynch, the narrative appears to slow down and the seasons seem to pause at their darkest moment. The feast day of the Church, rather than appearing in passing as it did in the earlier chapters, occurs at the end of the chapter, thereby seeming to bring some sense of spiritual climax to Stephen's life. His sins trickle from his lips at confession "in shameful drops from his soul festering and oozing like a sore, a squalid stream of vice" (*P* 144), thereby seeming to bring to an end the rhythm of Stephen's development.

If there was ever any doubt, however, that Stephen's destiny in *A Portrait* is bound by environment and experience, the beginning of the fourth chapter quickly dispels it. Though Stephen's life is still dominated by the religious life and his days are measured by the Church calendar—"Sunday was dedicated to the mystery of the Holy Trinity, Monday to the Holy Ghost, Tuesday . . ." (*P* 147)— the narrative again asserts its separate reality. The seasons still fall within a perceivable pattern and the flowing rhythm of Stephen's life, which appeared to trickle to a stop during the retreat, resumes its natural course. During the winter and approaching spring of Stephen's amended life, he feels, in spite of his scrupulous religious habits, "a flood slowly advancing towards his naked feet" and waits "for the first faint timid noiseless wavelet to touch his fevered skin" (*P* 152). In the waning hour of "the long summer daylight" (*P* 154), Stephen finally hears and knows he will reject the offer to study for the priesthood because he recognizes that after "so many years of order and obedience" he will now resist any effort of priest or his own "to end for ever, in time and in eternity, his freedom" (*P* 161–62).

There is an apparent pause in the narrative movement at the end of the fourth chapter, but the suspended moment of Stephen's epiphany, unlike the perverse attempt to defy experience in the previous chapter, is in perfect harmony with external reality. Stephen's discovery of his artistic mission, of the potential form in which his soul will express itself, shines forth in time and eternity. Knowing that he will never become a priest of the Church, he decides, at this supreme moment of his youth, to "create proudly out of the freedom and power of his soul, as the great artificer whose name he bore, a living thing, new and soaring and beautiful, impalpable, imperishable" (*P* 170).

A year has elapsed since the summer day before the start of Stephen's last year at Belvedere when he was offered the secret knowledge and power of the priesthood, but summer remains the season for Stephen's epiphany, which occurs just after he learns that he will be entering the university. The rhythmic pattern of tides that has reinforced and corresponded to the seasonal movement in *A Portrait* and, at times, even challenged Stephen during his moments of crisis and development now seems to surrender to Stephen's profound vision, which shines forth in the image of the seagirl he encounters while wading in a rivulet of the receding tidal waters. Stephen's epiphany, delivered out of the virgin womb of his own imagination, replaces the feast day of the Church and unfolds itself in the Dantean imagery of the soul as a wave-like flower spreading "in endless succession to itself, breaking in full crimson and unfolding and fading to palest rose, leaf by leaf and wave of light by wave of light, flooding all the heavens with its soft flushes, every flush deeper than the other" (*P* 172).

The brief pause in the narrative of *A Portrait*, as the soul discovers and celebrates its own self-sustaining rhythm, underlines the crucial importance of Stephen's epiphany, but it does not negate the importance of the world around him. At the moment when Stephen finally sees the potential of his soul in an image of beauty, he appears in perfect harmony with all that surrounds him. In other words, Stephen's vision appears transcendental, suspended beyond time because of its radiance and pristine source, but it is actualized within Stephen's world of experience—a truth Stephen will struggle against in *Ulysses* as he tries to reconcile the artist's imagination and the too often nightmarish reality of his life.

In the last chapter of *A Portrait* the narrative, now that Stephen's radiant vision has faded, assumes its separate course again. Rather than appearing to be in harmony with Stephen's soul, the narrative pattern now reinforces the ironic mode of the chapter by exposing Stephen's poverty and immaturity. Thus within the narrative frame of *A Portrait*, while Stephen may discover the true nature of his soul and know that his destiny is to express his discovery in artistic form, *A Portrait* ends with Stephen still a young man. While most of the final chapter, like the third and fourth, takes place within a few days, the narrative has already advanced through the disillusionment of the autumn and winter of Stephen's university career. We see him at the beginning of the chapter walking within a world of "rainladen trees" and "the strange wild smell of the wet leaves and bark" (*P* 176) that contrasts sharply with the squalor and confusion of his home. Now that Stephen possesses the knowledge of his soul, he resists the world more than ever, but, like it or not, his life still advances along its irresistible course, and the Church, which Stephen claims to serve no longer, still has its own order which acts insistently upon Stephen's life.

The narrative pattern now clearly exposes Stephen's dilemma at the end of *A Portrait*. While Stephen rejects the life of his family, nation, and religion and holds his knowledge of the true nature of his soul and destiny above the world around him, his Dublin life continues its inevitable movement and, accordingly, the feast days of the Church fall within their appointed pattern. Stephen may move to the rhythm of his own imagination, but the English class begins at ten whether he is there or not. The timeless moment of his villanelle, "pure as the purest water" (*P* 217) is interrupted by bird songs and bells; but a sudden memory of the day before completely shatters his composure. As he thinks of smoke rising from the whole earth in praise of his temptress, he sees in his mind's eye the earth "like a swinging smoking swaying censer, a ball of incense, an ellipsoidal ball" (P 218). Unfortunately for Stephen, the last image floats out of his memory of Moynihan's joke about the ellipsoidal balls of the cavalry, and ruins the enchantment of the moment. Stephen's long talk with Cranly, in which he declares that he will not serve, is dominated by his own need to confess his "sin" of refusing to make his Easter duty. As Cranly says, Stephen's mind is supersaturated with the religion in which he claims he no longer believes. In one of the novel's final ironies, we see the entries in Stephen's diary that run from March 20 to April 27, a time span that is almost identical to that for Easter, a moveable feast that falls on the first Sunday after the full moon or on any date between March 22 and April 25.[8]

Stephen's problem, his unresolved crisis at the end of A Portrait, is his unwillingness or failure to apply his knowledge of the soul to the life of experience around him in the same way he applies Aquinas to his aesthetic theories. He prefers to protect that knowledge from a life that threatens to fling nets at the soul "to hold it back from flight" (P 203). He will take his brief flight into exile to protect his soul against his enemies, but until he can transmute "the daily bread of experience into the radiant body of everliving life" (P 221), he will never become the priest of eternal imagination. That he is not ready at the end of A Portrait is reflected in the disharmony of Stephen's relationship with everyone around him and the ironic mode of the narrative itself.

The persistence of external reality in the narrative of A Portrait does not necessarily contradict those who have accepted Stephen's process of becoming as the sole reality of the novel and have found parallels between Joyce's technique and Bergsonian, Jungian, or Viconian thought.[9] Stephen's impressions of his experiences and his growing consciousness of historical and racial patterns are, without question, central to the novel. The world around Stephen, however, has its own ineluctable reality in A Portrait, its expression constantly lurking within the narrative itself. The narrative form of the novel, though it appears influenced by Bergsonian, Jungian, and Viconian thought, is clearly Aristotelian. Stephen's aesthetics may be applied Aquinas, but the narrative in *A Portrait* moves to the measure of applied Aristotle.

Joyce, who had gathered his own "garner of slender sentences from Aristotle's poetics and psychology" (*P* 176) for his aesthetic notebook and boasted to his friends that he was an Aristotelian,[10] found in Aristotle's definition of the soul the support he needed for his art in *A Portrait*. In *De Anima* Aristotle defines the soul as a substance which is the form or the essence or whatness of the body it animates.[11] He also states that the soul is bound to its body and the body is the means by which the soul expresses itself, whether in the form of passion, gentleness, fear, pity, courage, joy, loving, or hating. Translated in terms of the artist, form animates the work of art, which finds its means of expression in the daily bread of experience.[12] As the soul is free to express itself in time and space, so the artist's true freedom is bound within the same dimensions. Stephen's discovery of his soul, his form of forms, takes place in the world of actual experience and, no matter how he resists the unpleasant and threatening realities of growing up in Dublin, he will have to express his soul not vicariously through Hauptmann, Ibsen, or Cavalcanti but actually through his own living body.

Aristotle's principle of contradiction is also a determinant of the narrative movement and form of *A Portrait*. Stephen tells Lynch that "Aristotle's entire system of philosophy rests upon his book of psychology and that, I think, rests on his statement that the same attribute cannot at the same time and in the same connection belong to and not belong to the same subject" (*P* 208). It is also on the basis of this statement that, according to Richard Ellmann, "the non-subjective, external world" of Joyce's fiction "can be built up in unchallengeable thereness."[13] The external world, then, like the soul has its separate reality, but it is only through the soul as the form of forms that the world can be apprehended. The soul and the world, then, like form and content in a work of art, are inextricably bound with each other, for it is only within actual experience that the potentiality of the soul becomes realized and takes on the appearance of both inevitability and eternality.

Aristotle's division of the soul into potential and actual further reveals the nature of the relationship between the incorporeal and the corporeal, the soul and the world or body which function like the needle and thread of Aristotle's *De Anima*. Edmund Epstein notes that we can understand Joyce's definition of artistic freedom by following Aristotle's observations that the soul is the first entelechy of the body and that the second entelechy is the moment when the soul expresses itself in an exercise of some kind. The artist, then, has to go beyond the observation of "potential souls locked up in lumps of matter" to the apprehension of "the souls of men and things" in action to give "the creatures of his mind the same freedom that is enjoyed by natural creations."[14] Epstein, recognizing that Stephen's final ordeal is his struggle to advance to the second entelechy or state of actuality, argues that the conversations in the last chapter show Stephen's movement toward completeness. Stephen's reluctance, however, to accept his own soul as bound in time and space, like the basket of his aesthetic theories, and his subversion of the conversations into lectures and confessions argue for just the opposite view. In *A Portrait*, Stephen discovers his soul or the form of forms within the world around him but not until he weaves his theory of Shakespeare's artistry in the Scylla and Charybdis chapter in *Ulysses* will he begin to see a way in which he can express his discovery in an artistic form forged out of the gross materials of his life.

Aristotle's principle of apprehension offers a final measure of support for a reality external to Stephen's thoughts yet bound to his impressions. It also shows the way in which the artist builds a bridge between form and content, and it explains the impressionistic technique of *A Portrait* better than an excursion into either Dujardin or Bergson. Aristotle observed in *De Anima* that thinking and perceiving are often thought to be the same because "in the one as in the other the soul discriminates and is cognizant of something which *is*." Aristotle, however, found this view to be false because "perception of the special objects of sense is always free of error . . . while it is possible to think falsely." [15] Here is a revelation of the pure form of *A Portrait of the Artist as a Young Man*. Joyce's novel *is*, not because Stephen thinks but because Stephen perceives. The errors in Stephen's thinking that disturb so many readers do not reflect the essential form of *A Portrait*. Stephen's perceptions, his discovery of his soul and his knowledge that his mission is to create the uncreated conscience of his race, form the essence of the novel. Stephen's aesthetic evasion of the body of his experiences represents his youth, his fear that life, rather than being that in which he can express or actualize his soul, is the destructive element waiting to drown his soul.

The reason for the undeniable movement of the seasons and the irresistible rhythm of tides within and without in *A Portrait* is to assure us that the body of reality has its own identity. It is equally important to remember, however, that Stephen perceives the seasons and senses the tidal movements even when he misunderstands, misrepresents, or tries to evade their reality. *A Portrait* affirms the separate reality of the soul, its body, and the world's body by showing the way in which the artist discovers his essential whatness, his soul, within experience and learns that his mission is to create out of the body of life an image of eternity. Because Joyce's portrait is of the artist as a young man, we do not see, except in the form of the novel in our hands, this expression of the soul. When the artist has the maturity and power to express his soul, he can give the world a special meaning for himself and, if he can realize the value of his own soul in relation to others, a universal meaning as well. He can bind time and eternity, transmute the daily bread of experience into everliving life, and bring to us another feast day for our souls—a Bloomsday perhaps.

Notes

1. There is an excellent summary of the present state of scholarship in Thomas F. Staley's "Strings in the Labyrinth: Sixty Years with Joyce's *Portrait*," in *Approaches to*

Joyce's Portrait, ed. Thomas F. Staley and Bernard Benstock (Pittsburgh: Univ. of Pittsburgh Pr., 1976), pp. 3–24. See also Staley's essay, "James Joyce," in *Anglo-Irish Literature: A Review of Research*, ed. Richard J. Finneran (New York: Modern Language Association of America, 1976), pp. 402–10.

2. For a summary of the range of positions assumed by Joyce scholars in their study of *A Portrait*, see Chester G. Anderson's "Editor's Introduction," in *A Portrait of the Artist as a Young Man*, (New York: Viking, 1968), pp. 446–54.

3. See Hugh Kenner, "The *Portrait* in Perspective" in *A Portrait*, ed. Anderson, pp. 426, 439. Also see Kenner's "The Cubist *Portrait*," in *Approaches to Joyce's* Portrait, pp. 177–84.

4. Kenner, "The Cubist *Portrait*," p. 176.

5. *James Joyce* (New York: Oxford Univ. Pr., 1959), 307–9.

6. Edmund Epstein dates the section "about October ninth or tenth, 1891" and believes that Stephen's dream would be occurring at the same time that "Parnell's body was brought to Ireland on October 11, 1891." He also shows how Joyce "distorts both fictional and real chronology to effect a coincidence of little Stephen's rebellion and the death of Parnell." See *The Ordeal of Stephen Dedalus* (Carbondale: Southern Illinois Univ. Pr., 1971), pp. 36–37. For an attempt at a physical time-scheme, see Appendix A in Robert M. Adams, *James Joyce: Common Sense and Beyond* (New York: Random House, 1966), pp. 217–20.

7. This time the chronology of Joyce's life reinforces the time scheme of *A Portrait*. With the help of Father John Conmee, Joyce was able to enter Belvedere College on April 6, 1893. See Ellmann's *James Joyce*, p. 35, and Kevin Sullivan's *Joyce Among the Jesuits* (New York: Columbia Univ. Pr., 1958), p. 68. For Sullivan's comments on the chronological confusion of the third chapter, see pp. 124–26.

8. A riddle of "the man-in-the-macintosh" order is to fix the date of Easter from Stephen's diary entries. One intriguing possibility is to see the Thursday of the opening episode as Maundy Thursday (Stephen tells Lynch during their Thursday talk on aesthetics that Aquinas "wrote a hymn for Maundy Thursday" (*P* 210). This would date Stephen's confession to Cranly as Good Friday. This conversation, in turn, is recorded in the diary on March 20, apparently just after it has taken place. On the night of March 21, which would correspond to Easter Vigil, Stephen writes "Free. Soulfree and fancyfree. Let the dead bury the dead. Ay. And let the dead marry the dead" (*P* 248). Easter Sunday, then, would fall on March 22, the earliest possible date for Easter and the one which corresponds most closely with the vernal equinox. The entry in the diary, however, is anti-climactic: "In company with Lynch followed a sizable hospital nurse. Lynch's idea. Dislike it. Two lean hungry greyhounds walking after a heifer" (*P* 248).

9. The most comprehensive study of Bergsonian time and Joyce's art is in Shiv K. Kumar's *Bergson and the Stream of Consciousness Novel* (New York: New York Univ. Pr., 1963), pp. 103–38. The most extensive time studies of Joyce's fiction

have been those of Margaret Church. See, for example, *Time and Reality* (Chapel Hill: Univ. of North Carolina Pr., 1963), pp. 27–66.

10. Richard Ellmann offers a summary of Joyce's statements of admiration for Aristotle in *Ulysses on the Liffey* (New York: Oxford Univ. Pr., 1972), p. 12.

11. *The Basic Works of Aristotle*, ed. Richard McKeon (New York: Random House, 1941), pp. 555–56. In Joyce's 1903–1904 Notebook, he defines the soul as "the entelechy of a naturally organic body," as "the form of forms," and as "all that is."

12. In his Paris notebook for March 27, Joyce quotes from Aristotle, "*e tekhne mimeitai ten physin,*" and then comments, "This phrase is falsely rendered as 'Art is an imitation of Nature.' Aristotle does not here define art; he says only, 'Art imitates Nature' and means that the artistic process is like the natural process." *Workshop of Daedalus: James Joyce and the Raw Materials for* A Portrait of the Artist as a Young Man, ed. Robert Scholes and Richard M. Kain (Evanston, Ill.: Northwestern Univ. Pr., 1965), p. 54.

13. *Ulysses on the Liffey*, p. 17. Joyce, like Stephen, constructed his sense of time out of Aristotle's book of psychology, but Aristotle defines time in his Physics as the "'number of movement in respect of the before and after,' and is continuous since it is an attribute of what is continuous." (*The Basic Works of Aristotle*, p. 293). In *Ulysses*, Stephen thinks of movement as "an actuality of the possible as possible" (*U* 25).

14. *The Ordeal of Stephen Dedalus*, pp. 19–20.

15. *The Basic Works of Aristotle*, p. 587.

3

SHARI BENSTOCK AND BERNARD BENSTOCK

Ulysses: Narrative Movement and Placement

For some time now the narrative of *Ulysses*—what it is and how it works—has been of prime interest to students of Joyce's text. This interest has evidenced itself in a variety of workshops and panels at Joyce symposia and in dissertations, articles, notes, and book-length studies. The approaches to the narrative complexities of *Ulysses* have been varied, encompassing both close readings of the text such as those by David Hayman, Marilyn French, Roy Gottfried, and Herbert Schneidau, and more theoretical studies such as those by Wolfgang Iser, Franz Stanzel, André Topia, Jean-Michel Rabaté, John Paul Riquelme, and Brook Thomas. Our very particular interest pays special attention to the application of recent theoretical developments in German and French criticism to an analysis of certain components of the *Ulysses* narrative. We are concerned with problems of terminology (in identifying voices, sources of perception, narrative evidence) and of methodology (in accounting for parallel structures, textual intrusions, storytelling practices). Our work has been spurred by two critics whose words—both spoken and written—have profoundly changed our notions about this text: Fritz Senn and Hugh Kenner. Our debts to these two readers of *Ulysses* have little to do with whether we agree or disagree with their readings of the text, but rather with the ways they have made us look again at this narrative, question again the suppositions we held dear for many years, think again about Joyce's contribution to modern letters in *Ulysses*. The following article is part of a forthcoming book-length study.

The "omphalos" that figures as stage center of the opening chapter of *Ulysses* is at first the open top area of the Martello Tower in Sandycove to which Buck Mulligan summons up Stephen Dedalus and then calls him down. The tensions that exist between the two dominate their exchange in that confined space, but vast expanse of open air around them gives Stephen a certain degree of maneuverability, and he can look past his "threadbare cuffedge" (*U* 5) to the surrounding sea and the sky. Mulligan attempts to draw Stephen in, holding up a restrictive mirror for him to view himself, and even in this maneuver Stephen remains uncooperative, looking instead at the crack in the glass—like a "hair on end" (*U* 6). In the tight quarters of the gun emplacement Mulligan "linked his arm in Stephen's and walked with him round the tower" (*U* 7), and although they look "towards the blunt cape of Bray Head" (*U* 7), that outward objective can only be realized as an ideal: no one could be expected to see Bray Head from the Sandycove tower with the naked eye.

Left alone for a few minutes Stephen is far from the "moody brooding" (*U* 9) that Mulligan assumes. His mood is governed by the "morning peace" (*U* 9)—now that Mulligan has gone—and he gives himself over to the woodshadows and Yeats's song and the imagined sound of harpstrings. The freedom, however, proves shortlived: "A cloud began to cover the sun slowly" (*U* 9). And this oppressive presence weighs down upon him, changing his mood and returning his thoughts to his dead mother, so that Buck's call joins with the recurrence of sunshine as welcome relief: "Stephen, still trembling at his soul's cry, heard warm running sunlight and in the air behind him friendly words" (*U* 10). At the same time (although three chapters forward in the text) Leopold Bloom experiences the heavy weight of the same cloud. In the open street, where he purposely keeps to the "bright side" (*U* 57), the cloud catches him unaware: "A cloud began to cover the sun wholly slowly wholly" (*U* 61). His death thoughts reach their nadir of despair in "the grey sunken cunt of the world" (*U* 61), and he moves quickly toward home to the palliatives of food and Molly: "To smell the gentle smoke of tea, fume of the pan, sizzling butter. Be near her ample bedwarmed flesh" (*U* 61). Fortunately, sunshine, an avatar of Milly Bloom, rescues him while he is still in the open space of Eccles Street: "Quick warm sunlight came running from Berkeley Road, swiftly, in slim sandals, along the brightening footpath. Runs, she runs to meet me, a girl with gold hair on the wind" (*U* 61).

When Bloom is once again caught in the open by a cloud, he is moving toward lunch as previously he had been moving toward breakfast. He is smiling at the sun (at the idea of a "Home Rule sun rising up in the northwest"— *U* 164) when overtaken: "His smile faded as he walked, a heavy cloud hiding the sun slowly, shadowing Trinity's surly front" (*U* 164). Thoughts of lunacy, painful birth, omnipresent death, urban blight, and capitalist exploitation are blamed on the hour of the day, as previously they had been on getting up on the "wrong side of the bed" (*U* 61). This rationalization, however, is replaced by thoughts of "liver and bacon today" (*U* 164)—Molly no longer a soothing topic of thought—until the "sun freed itself slowly" (*U* 165) and stasis is recovered. An interceding moment of cloudiness, equidistant in time between these two, occurs in Hades, when Bloom puts his head out of the carriage window at the Grand Canal. There is no indication of Bloom's awareness of the change, but his view of the gasworks while on the way to Dignam's burial is sufficient to conjure up thoughts of illness and death, until a "raindrop spat on his hat" (*U* 90). He takes this meteorological change in stride ("—The weather is changing, he said quietly"— *U* 90), and is entertained by Simon Dedalus's witticism ("as uncertain as a child's bottom"— *U* 90). In this instance he is securely cocooned among his companions, closed off in the snug carriage, and even if Dedalus, Cunningham and Power are hardly his friends, they serve for the moment as well as Mulligan's "friendly" voice had served for Stephen.

Stephen's descent into the tower in Telemachus brings him into his most claustrophic position, both in regard to Mulligan and Haines. The bowels of the battlement are a Dantean inferno ("Janey Mack, I'm choked. He howled without looking up from the fire"— *U* 11), and it is Stephen, the temporary keeper of the key, who opens the heavy door: "welcome light and bright air entered" (*U* 11). Even the sanctity of Stephen's mind has been invaded by Mulligan, especially in this chapter of "close quarters": the scene in Clive Kempthorpe's Oxford rooms derives from Mulligan's experiences which are now "rethought" by Stephen Dedalus, who rescues himself from the dangers of entrapment by moving outward through the open window to where a deaf gardener moves freely, indifferent to the ragging within. Mulligan's voice in particular rummages about with abandon in Stephen's thoughts in self-advertisement ("God, we'll simply have to dress the character. I want puce gloves and green boots"—*U* 17) and in self-aggrandizement ("He wants that key. It is mine, I paid the rent"—*U* 20). As Arnold Goldman maintains, it is Mulligan who asserts that he rented the tower, and Stephen is "hearing" Mulligan say so. In Lotus Eaters Bloom takes temporary refuge in All Hallows, where he can be "alone" with his thoughts. Those thoughts, of course, are often about Molly, and as he sits in the pew he reads the letters on the officiating priest's "back" from his vantage to the side, so that the left side of the priest's back is more visible: "I.N.R.I.? No: I.H.S." (*U* 81). He goes on to spell out the acronym: "Molly told me one time I asked her. I have sinned: or no: I have suffered, it is. And the other one? Iron nails ran in" (*U* 81). These classic examples of Bloom's ignorance of Catholicism may not be his own; he may be quoting Molly verbatim on both I.H.S. and I.N.R.I., her voice now echoing precisely within his mind.

The third "scene" of Telemachus completes the descent from the tower and out onto the swimming area, just as the third "scene" of Lotus Eaters takes Bloom back out through the front door of the church to Westland Row. For Stephen the freedom of open space is only a foretaste of complete freedom from Mulligan and the tower ("I will not sleep here tonight," Stephen decides—*U* 23), and in the open air he is relatively free of Mulligan's taunts and accusations, and his friendly entrapments. No longer "displeased and sleepy" (*U* 3), Stephen expands sufficiently to take all in stride, and liberally pronounces his maledictions on Haines—"Horn of a bull, hoof of a horse, smile of a Saxon"—and on Mulligan: "Usurper" (*U* 23). For Bloom the church interior was a sanctuary rather than a confining space, away from the casual intrusions which the streets of Dublin so easily afford. As he was accosted by M'Coy prior to his visit to All

Hallows, so is he accosted once he has gone out. No sooner has he walked the length of the short street to Sweny's than Bantam Lyons waylays him outside that establishment; and if Clive Hart is correct in his supposition, it may not have been a chance encounter: Lyons may have been in Conway's pub, have spotted Bloom carrying a newspaper, and purposely set his sights on having a free look at the *Freeman's Journal*. The open streets are treacherous for Leopold Bloom, and he navigates carefully at all times ("He crossed to the bright side, avoiding the loose cellarflap of number seventyfive"— *U* 57); Hugh Kenner has commented that *Ulysses* is a survival manual for the urban dweller.

The second and third chapters of the Telemachia expand the internal-constricting/external-expansive possibilities for Stephen Dedalus. In Nestor he is once again the uncomfortable animal in a cage, and although in a commanding position over his pupils Stephen has no real control over them. A permissive teacher turning a blind eye on the petty dishonesties of his upper middle-class students, he achieves something of a standoff at best, commiserating and identifying with Cyril Sargeant, the two of them left behind while the other students dash off to the playing field. Then even Sargeant is liberated and runs off to play hockey, while Stephen is ensnared by Mr. Deasy, his employer and paymaster, for whom he has to wait. ("Stale smoky air hung in the study with the smell of drab abraded leather of its chairs" [*U* 29] parallels the smoke-filled inner confines of the Martello tower.) Their transaction is of course delayed by Deasy's holding forth on home economics and foreign policy, while from the vast outdoors the liberated cries of the hockey players offer an obvious contrast: "Hooray! Ay! Whrrwhee!" (*U* 34). And even after Stephen goes "out by the open porch and down the gravel path under the trees" (*U* 35), Deasy shouts after him, tugging him back with his belated witticism.

In Proteus Stephen achieves a measure of liberation, alone and in the open, yet inwardly confined with the flotsam and jetsam of his mind. Externally he is his own man, and even his bodily functions are satisfied *en plein air*; by contrast Bloom holes himself up in his backyard jakes, a "king" in his "counting house" (*U* 68), "restraining himself" in his bowel movement (*U* 69), but with "the door ajar" (*U* 68). Bloom seems to gravitate naturally toward enclosed areas, despite having consciously chosen a profession that keeps him out of office confinement, while Stephen seems to thrive on getting out of enclosures. In his imagination Stephen "visits" the residence of his maternal uncle, a house under siege by creditors ("They take me for a dun, peer out from a coign of vantage"—*U* 38), but when it comes actually to turning into Strasburg Terrace, he lets the thought serve for the deed: "He halted. I have passed the way to aunt Sara's. Am I not going there? Seems not" (*U* 41). Although he can imagine the visit in minute detail from previous experiences, he chooses to pass by the house (and the chance of a possible night's lodging) with a conscious decision—"This wind is sweeter" (*U* 39).

We can only speculate on what Stephen is doing on Sandymount Strand in Proteus and how he got there. The time that has elapsed since the end of the previous chapter is not enough to allow for his having walked all the way, yet if he took the train, why not all the way into Dublin, his ultimate destination? The urban center is his natural habitat and performance stage (in *A Portrait* the move into the city coincides with Stephen's coming of age), yet he is apprehensive; in the newspaper office he will muse, "Dublin. I have much, much to learn" (*U* 144). If Stephen has intentionally interrupted his trip into the city for a brief respite along the strand (rather than a stop at the Gouldings), he may well have availed himself of the most tranquil hour of his day, yet not without certain perils. The rhythmic movements of the sea lull his thoughts, determining the rhythms of his thinking as well as the rhythms of his aimless peregrinations. Deprived of an immediate destination (Strasburg Terrace) and loath to commit himself to an announced destination ("—The Ship, Buck Milligan cried. Half twelve"—*U* 23), he is drawn out toward the sea:

He had come nearer the edge of the sea and wet sand slapped his boots. The new air greeted him, harping in wild nerves, wind of wild air of seeds of brightness. Here, I am not walking out to the Kish lightship, am I? He stood suddenly, his feet beginning to sink slowly in the quaking soil. Turn back.

Turning, he scanned the shore south, his feet sinking again slowly in new sockets. (*U* 44)

Movement forward brings the hydrophobe Stephen dangerously close to the realm of the drowned man; a cessation of movement causes him to sink downward into the sand.

The Stephen of Proteus, acknowledging "I am not a strong swimmer" (*U* 45), has moved close to the edge of the briny deep, endangering himself like Hippolytus ("Vehement breath of waters amid seasnakes, rearing horses, rocks"—*U* 49), or like Lycidas ("Sunk though he be beneath the watery floor"—*U* 50), and is lulled into thinking of his own demise by water as a "Seadeath, mildest of all deaths known to man" (*U* 50). To teach "Lycidas" in the safe bounds of a schoolhouse in Dalkey is now translated into experiencing Lycidas's seadeath where the drowned man has had his demise, and is now a "Bag of corpsegas sopping in foul brine" (*U* 50). Even the recollection of a bowl of still water proves discomfiting (as had the "bowl of white china" [*U* 5] in which his dying mother had vomited): "When I put my face into it in the basin at Clongowes. Can't see! Who's behind me? Out quickly, quickly!" (*U* 45). His reflection in the basin draws him into himself, as he had realized with Mulligan's cracked lookingglass, making him vulnerable from without.

Bloom's wanderings in Lotus Eaters eventually lead him to the lulling baths, the ablutions prior to the Dignam burial. He meanders (purposely? purposeless?) through the southeastern quarter of Dublin, perhaps throwing off anyone who might be tailing him, claiming Martha's letter at the Westland Row post office and buying soap at Sweny's, temporarily arrested by M'Coy and Lyons. (As Clive Hart has noticed, his peregrinations form a pair of interrogation marks on the map of the city.) His thoughts appear aimless, but not particularly troubled as yet: his destination in time is the 11 A.M. funeral, in space the baths on Tara Street. The establishment had already connoted an element of escape for Bloom, even before he set out on his mysterious trek: in Calypso he thinks, "Wonder have I time for a bath this morning. Tara Street. Chap in the paybox there got away James Stephens they say. O'Brien" (*U* 68). (That the cashier at the baths may have been involved in the prison break of the Fenian head-centre parallels speculation that the counter man at the cabman's shelter drove the decoy cab for the Invincibles after the Phoenix Park murders.) Despite his announced intentions Bloom does not frequent the Tara Street baths, but goes to the ones on Leinster Street instead. In a chapter that specializes in deflected movements (the longest way to Westland Row is through Tara Street; in the back door of All Hallows, out the front), anyone looking for Bloom in the Tara Street baths will be disappointed.

As a pedestrian Bloom takes his tentative stroll in Calypso, around the corner to Dorset Street for a pork kidney, veering toward the west (bright) side of Eccles, past the barely friendly sentinel on the corner (Larry O'Rourke), and into the haven offered by Dlugacz the pork butcher. There he is tempted by an even friendlier haven, a return to a Palestinian homeland advertised as Agendath Netaim, but a siren in the form of the nextdoor maid almost leads him astray ("To catch up and walk behind her if she went slowly"— *U* 59). Not only does she go off in the opposite direction (she "sauntered lazily to the right"—*U* 59), but once he is outside Bloom cannot find her ("No sign. Gone. What matter?"), and he walks "back along Dorset Street" (*U* 60), where he encounters the menace of a dark cloud; now neither side of the street is bright. The excursion to the jakes—a tight enclosure within the outer enclosure of his garden wall, with the door left comfortingly ajar—provides a few moments of solace for him.

The respite in All Hallows, and presumably the wallowing in the public bath, are Bloom's most secure moments in Lotus Eaters, while the encapsulation in the carriage contrasts with public exposure at Glasnevin cemetery. Although slighted both on entering and leaving the carriage (the last one in and the last out), he seems to feel nicely contained: he can spot Stephen even when Simon Dedalus does not, and he can ignore Boylan by gazing at his nails; he can retreat inside himself when the painful subject of suicide is discussed, and although he fails to tell the Reuben J. Dodd anecdote very well, he is unconcerned when it is taken away from him by Cunningham. After all, it was only a dodge to deflect away from his difference from the others, Bloom never having recourse to moneylenders. At Glasnevin, however, the open terrain again leaves Bloom vulnerable, and the other three can now discuss him behind his back. Even solicitation proves uncomfortable when Tom Kernan attaches himself to him, Bloom being neither a good enough Catholic or Protestant to deal readily with the situation. And Menton's snub caps the discomforts of the occasion.

An aspect of survival for Bloom has been the ability to control the doors that are his means of ingress and egress, not just the "crazy door of the jakes" (*U* 68), but his front door as well. Keyless throughout the day, his first ploy when going out to the butcher's is to manipulate the appearance of his house door: "He pulled the halldoor to after him very quietly, more, till the footleaf dropped gently over the threshold, a limp lid. Looked shut. All right till I come back anyhow" (*U* 57). In Aeolus, however, doors operate outside of Bloom's volition; in this chapter, movement is governed by cross-current winds ("They always build one door opposite another for the wind to. Way in. Way out"—*U* 117), a process inherent in the printing machines that move relentlessly in and out, forward and back: "The machines clanked in threefour time. . . . Now if he got paralysed there and no one knew how to stop them they'd clank on and on the same, print it over and over and up and back" (*U* 119). The rhythmic language of Aeolus follows the same self-reflexive/self-retractive action ("Grossbooted draymen rolled barrels dull-thudding out of Prince's stores and bumped them up on the brewery float. On the brewery float bumped dullthudding barrels rolled by grossbooted draymen out of Prince's stores"—*U* 116). Although Bloom is particularly sensitive to the mechanical movement, he is nonetheless subject to its laws. As he analyzes the process: "Sllt. The nethermost deck of the first machine jogged forwards its flyboard with sllt the first batch of quirefolded papers. Sllt. Almost human

the way it sllt to call attention. Doing its level best to speak. That
door too sllt creaking, asking to be shut. Everything speaks in its
own way. Sllt" (*U* 121). Bloom's manipulation of doors breaks down
in Aeolus, despite his ability to "speak their language," and venturing into the *Evening Telegraph* office to use the telephone places him
in a tight box ("The doorknob hit Mr Bloom in the small of the back
as the door was pushed in"—*U* 124). This collision with J. J.
O'Molloy is duplicated when Bloom comes through a door and
bumps against Lenehan: "—My fault, Mr Bloom said, suffering his
grip. Are you hurt?" (*U* 129).

Although the newspaper offices are Bloom's familiar working
areas, he is buffeted about in a series of closed boxes, rooms in which
doors are mysterious and dangerous. In the streets of Dublin he can
guide Josie Breen clear of Cashel Boyle O'Connor Fitsmaurice
Tisdall Farrell's maniacal stride and help a blind stripling across the
street, but he is helpless in the halls of the winds, where newsboys
are pushed through doors ("It was Pat Farrel shoved me, sir"—*U*
128); and once Bloom escapes—the curses of Myles Crawford echoing after him—the newsboys follow him down the street and mock
his walk. Stephen, on the other hand, slithers in and out with ease:
the rhythmic movement operates faultlessly as Dedalus *père* manages
to sllt out before Dedalus *fils* sllts in, the two never bumping into
each other. Whether Stephen comes to the *Telegraph* office volun-
tarily (he is, after all, an errand boy for Deasy on this occasion), he
adjusts comfortably to the situation, having bypassed his appoint-
ment with Mulligan at the Ship. Instead he recommends another
pub, offers to stand drinks, and leads a contingent of five out into the
street, narrating his parable along the way. But the open-ended possibilities of O'Connell Street defeat his purpose: he can command
the absolute attention of only one (limited) auditor, Professor
McHugh. Two of the others are in advance of them ("Lenehan and
Mr O'Madden Burke, hearing, turned, beckoned and led on across
towards Mooney's"—*U* 148), although all six had started out together. The parable begins *in camera*, is continued down the stairs to
the disruptive rhythm of a "bevy of scampering newsboys" who rush

"down the steps, scampering in all directions" (*U* 146)—while O'Molloy is simultaneously trying to borrow money from Crawford—and presumably ends in the middle of tram-crammed O'Connell Street, "on sir John Gray's pavement island" (*U* 150). Stephen's narrative oddly ends *in medias res*.

Stephen fares somewhat better in Lyster's office at the National Library, where the four walls contain the listeners to his Shakespeare disquisition. The office door, however, allows for several interruptions: George Russell escapes a third of the way through and Buck Mulligan invades a third of the way from the end of Stephen's performance. In addition, the Quaker librarian, his most polite and attentive hearer, is twice called out by library clients, one of whom is Bloom himself, who had interrupted the parable in Crawford's office by his intrusion there. It is fitting irony that Stephen should have the opportunity to repeat his parable with Bloom as sole listener in the Eccles Street kitchen, yet lose his attention when the parable title, *A Pisgah Sight of Palestine* (this time offered in advance of the narrative), apparently evokes a separate line of thoughts in Bloom's mind, the Moses allusions making him think of "essays on various subjects or moral apothegms (e.g. *My Favourite Hero* or *Procrastination is the Thief of Time*)" (*U* 685).

Once Bloom has returned from Glasnevin, the goal of his morning, he throws himself into his work (the newspaper offices) and avoids as much as possible troublesome thoughts of Molly and Boylan—but these prove unavoidable. His walk down Westmoreland and Grafton Streets is determined by his desire for lunch, the hot food that will supplant the bedwarmed flesh that had been his previous haven ("Hope they have liver and bacon today"—*U* 164). Just as everything he sees and everyone he meets will revert the subject to Molly, so the hot lunch eludes him: the Burton proves too disgusting, and he settles for a cold sandwich at Davy Byrne's. Bracketed between the publican and Nosey Flynn, an old acquaintance, he is relatively secure within the pub, until Flynn mentions Blazes Boylan: "A warm shock of air heat of mustard hauched on Mr Bloom's heart. He raised his eyes and met the stare of a bilious clock. . . .

Not yet" (*U* 172–73). From this moment on the relentless movement of time brings him toward the instant of the Molly-Blazes assignation, and it becomes the marker for him until four o'clock: "Afternoon she said" (*U* 183); "At four she. . . . Ternoon" (*U* 264). Once he leaves the moral pub Bloom is masterfully in control of Molesworth Street, guiding the blind piano tuner across the intersecting Dawson Street; but at the other end, at the Kildare Street intersection, he almost meets his doom: Boylan walking south toward their inevitable point of impact. From his sanctuary in the funeral carriage he avoided eye contact ("Mr Bloom reviewed the nails of his left hand, then those of his right hand"—*U* 92), but now in the open street he can only rush across Kildare, trusting to the sun in Boylan's eyes, and dash through the museum gate, all the while pretending to be preoccupied in searching for something in his pockets, until he can declare himself "Safe!" (*U* 183).

The third time proves a fatal charm: at four o'clock, from across the Liffey Bloom notices Boylan's jaunting car heading toward the Ormond Hotel: "He eyed and saw afar on Essex bridge a gay hat riding on a jauntingcar. It is. Third time. Coincidence" (*U* 263). Unable to resist the temptation, Bloom crosses the river and follows Boylan, stationing himself in the dining room of the Ormond where he can observe Boylan at the bar. Spatial relationships provide Bloom with a strategic vantagepoint in the closed complex of restaurant, bar, and saloon, where sound waves carry the songs sung by Simon Dedalus and Ben Dollard, and imagined transmittal of sound the jingle of Boylan's departing car long after it is out of earshot— "Jingle a tinkle jaunted" (*U* 267); "Jiggedy jingle jaunty jaunty" (*U* 271); "Jingle jaunty" (*U* 273); "Jingle by monuments of sir John Gray" (*U* 276); "Jingle into Dorset street" (*U* 277)—until "Jog jig jogged stopped" (*U* 282) and Boylan is "heard" knocking at 7 Eccles Street: "a loud proud knocker, with a cock carracarracarra cock. Cockcock" (*U* 282). Wavelengths extend beyond immediate hearing; thought waves violate all boundaries, of the walls of library rooms and the walls of Stephen's head as his thoughts on "a rosery of Fetter Lane of Gerard, herbalist" (*U* 202) are wafted (slightly transmuted) into the sirens atmosphere of the Ormond: "In Gerard's rosery of Fetter lane" (*U* 280). Bloom's idea that "Everything speaks in its own way" (*U* 121) is carried forward into the Sirens chapter: "Understand animals too that way. Solomon did. Gift of nature./ Ventriloquise. My lips closed. Think in my stom. What?" (*U* 285). His stomach does indeed speak as he walks away from the Ormond. Flatulence competes with Bloom's silent reading of Emmet's last speech to the court, timed to coincide with a noisy tram:

Nations of the earth. No-one behind. She's passed. *Then and not till then.* Tram. Kran, kran, kran. Good oppor. Coming. Krandlkrankran. I'm sure it's the burgund. Yes. One, two. *Let my epitaph be.* Karaaaaaaa. *Written. I have.*
Pprrpffrrppffff.
Done. (*U* 291)

The open streets, the domain of wandering rocks, could be per-ilous, and Stephen Dedalus, having encountered his pathetic sister Dilly at the bookstalls, spends most of his free afternoon in pubs ("Mooney's en ville, Mooney's sur mer, the Moira, Larchet's"—*U* 518) until we again discover him in the Holles Street Hospital. Bloom, in the interim, has made the mistake of venturing into Barney Kiernan's public house, instead of waiting safely outside for Cunningham and Power. Safe in Davy Bryne's and the Ormond as a diner, the non-drinker is vulnerable in the lair of the drinkers. His natural enemy, the Citizen (who under ordinary circumstances can be counted on to remain solidly on his pub stool), spots him imme-diately outside: "—What's that bloody freemason doing, says the citizen, prowling up and down outside?" (*U* 300). Once inside hos-tile territory he also makes the mistake of venturing out again, so that speculation can arise about his absence: "He had a few bob on *Throwaway* and he's gone to gather in the shekels" (*U* 335). When he next returns ("—I was just round at the courthouse, says he, looking for you"—*U* 341), the Citizen's vehemence breaks forth and Bloom is rushed out of the trap and into a jaunting car, but even the streets by now are no longer safe. The aroused onlookers ("all the ragamuffins and sluts of the nation round the door"—*U* 342) join in the invective, and no area of Dublin seems secure for Bloom. His departure in great haste will be replicated by Stephen's rushing out of Bella Cohen's some seven hours later. The coming of darkness late on a mid-June night changes the spatial relationships and enforces its own rhythms. In Nausicaa, Bloom and Gerty MacDowell carefully arrange a safe distance but adequate proximity to each other, a territorial separation violated accidentally by the children's ball and purposely by the insensitive Cissy Caffrey intent on asking the time: "So over she went and when he saw her coming she could see him take his hand out of his pocket, getting nervous, and beginning to play with his watchchain" (*U* 361). At the established distance Bloom is a handsome and tragic stranger and Gerty a delicate and demure damsel, a relationship that is expected to endure, protected by night falling. Gerty obviously hopes to effect her escape under cover of darkness, so that her telltale limp will not be noticed, but the night is not yet dark enough and Bloom discovers her secret—as presumably she had known of his, the secret masturbation under the protective covering of his clothes and insufficient light. Probably aware that the "distance" between them had been transgressed upon, Gerty moves off "Slowly without looking back" (*U* 367).

The rainclouds that burst later in the evening inundate Mulligan and Bannon, but leave Bloom and Stephen unscathed in the warm womb of the hospital Common Room, where both remain relatively protected from abuse. The ten medical students and hangers-on are fixed in proximate relationship around the table (once the two rain-soaked newcomers join them, and allowing for Dr. Dixon called away for the birth), but once they decide to move off for last drinks at the nearest pub, space becomes fluid. They attempt to keep in formation, starting out "armstrong, hollering down the street" (*U* 424), someone even dictating a military regularity: "March! Tramp, tramp the boys are (attitudes!) parching" (*U* 424). But Dixon is feeling ill and lagging behind ("Hurrah there, Dix"—*U* 424), probably accompanied by Punch Costello ("Where's Punch"—*U* 424). Stephen undoubtedly stands out alone, attracting the attention of the local street urchins ("Jay, look at the drunken minister coming out of the maternity hospal!"—*U* 424), and Bloom, also somewhat apart from the arm-strong cluster, moves them aside and earns an invitation to the pub: "Righto, Isaacs, shove em out of the bleeding limelight. Yous join uz, dear sir?" (*U* 424). But the doorway of Burke's frustrates any attempt by a phalanx to gain simultaneous entrance, and what began as a military formation disintegrates into a rugby scrimmage: "Heave to. Rugger. Scrum in. No touch kicking. Wow, my tootsies! You hurt? Most amazingly sorry!" (*U* 425).

The Burke's enclosure swallows the ten new customers, and the loose-knit entity distributes itself along the counter for drinks. The narrative medium approximates radio transmission, sound without vision, and only the "voices" of the ten are heard in clusters along the bar, the groupings only hinted at by narrative interaction. Stephen, buying the drinks, is very much in his element, and Bloom, for whom a pub had previously been near-disaster, remains secure, despite his choice of ginger cordial ("Chase me, the cabby's caudle"— *U* 425), and dominates sufficiently to frighten Bannon into a hasty exit: "Bloo? Cadges ads? Photo's papli, by all that's gorgeous! Play low, pardner. Slide. *Bonsoir la compagnie*" (*U* 427). A similar radio/non-video transmittal is operative on a lesser scale in Eumaeus, where the denizens of the cabman's shelter are rather shadowy customers: Bloom and Stephen clearly defined; the keeper and the sailor perhaps sailing under false colors as Fitzharris and Murphy; and the remaining three thoroughly indistinct (jarvies? longshoremen? loafers?). One of the three undergoes dim transformations before our eyes, from bearing "a distant resemblance to Henry Campbell, the townclerk" (*U* 631) to having "really quite a look of Henry Campbell" (*U* 638), to being "the cabby like Campbell, facial blemishes apart" (*U* 641) and "the *soi-disant* townclerk Henry Campbell" (*U* 650). Stephen, who had been quite expansive outside in lavishing a half-crown on Corley, becomes withdrawn and uncommunicative inside with Bloom, until they begin their departure and Bloom seems to earn a modicum of Stephen's respect by answering the simple and basic question of why "they put tables upside down at night, I mean chairs upside down on the tables in cafes" (*U* 660). Once outside Stephen even allows Bloom to narrow the space between them: "he passed his left arm in Stephen's right and led him on accordingly" (*U* 660). As they saunter off, Stephen sings to him, and the two look strangely like a married couple "Side by side" (*U* 665).

The intervening experiences in Nighttown are controlled by the transformational magic whose rhythm "jerks on" like the Idiot (*U* 429), or marches "unsteadily rightaboutface" like Privates Carr and Compton (*U* 430), or "climbs in spasms" like Tommy Caffrey (*U* 433), or is "staggering forward" like the drunken navvy (*U* 433)—no respector of fixed forms or marked distances. As Stephen's guardian angel Bloom nonetheless is constantly in danger on the streets and in Bella Cohen's, suffering numerous changes from the heights of being Lord Mayor to the depths of being Bello's Miss Ruby. But it is Stephen who confidently enters Nighttown to become its victim: in the confined parlour of the brothel he encounters the ghost of his mother, and after smashing the lamp, rushes out to the safety of the streets, where he encounters the wrath of Private Carr. Only the final transformation (Bloom as Yeats's Fergus, Stephen as Bloom's Rudy) offers a fleeting instant of equilibrium for Stephen, the enduring stasis to be worked out later in the kitchen and back garden of 7 Eccles Street.

The road to Eccles Street has its hazards ("—Our lives are in peril tonight. Beware of the steamroller"—*U* 662), but once they have circumvented the horse turds and stepped over the chain, Bloom and Stephen survive easily by following "parallel courses" (*U* 666). The communion that brings them together in Bloom's kitchen—after the keyless citizen gains access to his citadel—is culminated in the open space under the stars, "the infinite lattiginous scintillating uncondensed milky way, discernible by daylight by an observer placed at the lower end of a cylindrical vertical shaft 5000 ft deep sunk from the surface towards the centre of the earth" (*U* 698). Stephen goes off homeless into infinite space; Bloom goes in home-bound into finite and cramped quarters: in Cyclops the biscuit tin had flown by him "like a shot off a shovel" (*U* 345) without injuring its intended victim, but inside his safe house the navigator of Dublin's dangerous streets has the "right temporal lobe of the hollow sphere of his cranium" come "into contact with a solid timber angle" (*U* 705); the furnishings of his familiar terrain have been moved in his absence. Nonetheless, all roads that had led to home continue to lead Sinbad's companion to that closed space of sleep—positioned in a circle with Molly head to foot in their bed—that round black filled circle that is the element of closure in Ithaca. In a parallel course, but separated by a lapsed hour of time, Molly makes the same progression within the enclosed area she had rarely left during the entire day, and more specifically in the closed realm of her infinite thoughts —where the Rock of Gibraltar with Mulvey ("I was a Flower of the mountain yes"—*U* 783) occupies the same locus as the Hill of Howth with Bloom ("I was a flower of the mountain yes—*U* 782). Molly Bloom in her night thoughts, bound in a nutshell, is a queen of infinite space—as she enters the world of dreams.

4

PATRICK A. McCARTHY

"A Warping Process": Reading *Finnegans Wake*

> At the nearest licensed counter [Mick Shaughnessy] studied the amber
> charm of a glass of whiskey and made up his mind once again that he
> must behave himself. *Finnegans Wake*, though, and all that line of
> incoherent trash be damned! What was the teaching of the Church on
> this question of literary depravity? He did not know but perhaps he
> could find out from one of those little Catholic Truth Society pamphlets,
> price tuppence.
>
> —Flann O'Brien, *The Dalkey Archive*

Commenting briefly but perceptively on James Joyce's habit of shocking the reader of *Ulysses* by changing the book's style with each new chapter, one critic recently has argued that Joyce's reader "takes on an aspect suspiciously close to that of martyr—or masochist."[1] If we are thus moved to pity the reader of *Ulysses*, or perhaps to admire him or her for attempting an heroic journey comparable to those described by Homer and by Joyce, then how much more sympathy and admiration should we feel for the foolhardy readers of *Finnegans Wake*, who find their efforts at comprehension mocked by the very book they are reading? What is the tone of a passage like "You is feeling like you was lost in the bush, boy? You says: It is a puling sample jungle of woods. You most shouts out: Bethicket me for a stump of a beech if I have the poultriest notions what the farest he all means" (*FW* 112.3–6): does Joyce here reveal his compassion for the reader's plight, or his derision and contempt, or merely his profound sense of the ironic? Regardless of Joyce's intentions, an address of this kind, combined with the punning language, the obscure narrative situation, and complex problems in characterization, might be enough to convince us that the book is as "usylessly unreadable" as Shem's letter (*FW* 179.26–27) had Joyce not also counseled patience, reminded us to be alert for what we can hear as well as what we see, and assured us that the book "is not a miseffectual whyacinthinous riot of blots and blurs and bars and balls and hoops and wriggles and juxtaposed jottings linked by spurts of speed: it only looks as like it as damn it" (*FW* 118.28–31).

One thing is clear: no book since *Tristram Shandy* demonstrates its author's concern with tricking, manipulating, and toying with its readers so incessantly as *Finnegans Wake*. The comparison with Sterne's comic masterpiece was in fact suggested by Joyce himself: telling Eugene Jolas that he was "trying to build many planes of narrative with a single esthetic purpose," he added, rather pointedly, "Did you ever read Laurence Sterne?"[2] Like *Tristram Shandy*, *Finnegans Wake* works on several levels at once, and Joyce challenges his readers to discover the relationship between one level and another; like Sterne, who declares that his "work is digressive, and it is progressive too,———and at the same time,"[3] Joyce eschews "wideawake language, cutanddry grammar and goahead plot" (*L* III, 146). Both writers thus make unusual demands of their readers, and both are aware of the ironies inherent not only in the burdens they place on readers but also in their own roles as mentors or guides through their labyrinthine fictions. As penance for her failure to realize that Tristram's mother was not a papist, Sterne (or, rather, Tristram) sentences his hypothetical female reader to review the previous chapter; while she is gone he addresses himself to the remainder of his audience, defending his action on the grounds that it was necessary "to rebuke a vicious taste which has crept into thousands besides herself,———of reading straight forwards, more in quest of the adventures, than of the deep erudition and knowledge which a book of this cast, if read over as it should be, would infallibly impart with them."[4] Typically, too, Joyce's readers find themselves lectured by someone posing as an omniscient narrator (although the tendency of this lecturer to speak in the bourgeois voice of Shaun renders his authority dubious), and in the process of reading *Finnegans Wake*, even more than in reading *Ulysses*, we continually find ourselves searching for other appearances of a character, theme, or verbal motif in order to shed some light on the passage at hand. Reading *Finnegans Wake*, then, consists partly of locating cross-references and making marginal notes on what we have discovered this time around. For the most part, those people who do not like to write in their books do not bother with the *Wake*.

C. S. Lewis has observed that "The first qualification for judging any piece of workmanship from a corkscrew to a cathedral is to know *what* it is—what it was intended to do and how it is meant to be used."[5] The debate over what *Finnegans Wake* really is, and what Joyce intended it to be, is hardly over: Sheldon Brivic even claims—with some justification—that "questions about the *Wake* seem to be increasing."[6] There is little doubt, however, that *Finnegans Wake* is a fine example (in fact, the ultimate example) of what semioticians have called the *open*, or *plural*, text. Such a text is meant to be "generated" by the reader through a sort of cooperative venture with the author; as Umberto Eco puts it, "the 'original' text [is] a flexible *type* of which many *tokens* can be legitimately realized."[7] The open text, then, gives the impression of being deliberately incomplete, of having "gaps" which elicit a response from the reader who must fill in those gaps by resorting to any of a number of strategies (for example, by bringing a body of knowledge to bear upon the text, by recognizing a relationship of part to part within the text, or by analyzing the text from a carefully narrowed point of view). Finding ourselves "lost in the bush," we regain our bearings just in time to become disoriented again, for every new fact must be assimilated into our total interpretation of the text—an interpretation that is inevitably unstable, that (like our composite view of the universe) derives its sense of order only from a careful selection of those facts that support the hypothesis we have in mind at any time.

Although this disorientation of the reader is more evident in *Finnegans Wake* than in other works, it is a factor in much of modern literature—in Virginia Woolf's novels, for example, and in the works of such *nouveau roman* writers as Alain Robbe-Grillet. Iser has noted the same effect in Beckett's fiction:

Beckett's trilogy deprives the reader not temporarily but totally of his usual privileged seat in the grandstand. These characters possess a degree of self-consciousness which the reader can scarcely, if at all, keep up with. Such texts act as irritants, for they refuse to give the reader any bearings by means of which he might move far enough away to judge them. The text forces him to find his own way around, provoking questions to which he must supply his own answers.[8]

Nothing could be closer to the situation of the reader in *Finnegans Wake*, if we substitute the self-consciousness of the *book* for that of the *characters*. To a large extent *Finnegans Wake* is a running commentary on itself—how it came to be written, what its implications are about the nature of time, space, history, dream psychology, etc., and what problems the reader faces in grappling with Joyce's "wholemole millwheeling vicociclometer" (*FW* 614.27). The self-consciousness, or reflexivity, of the book is apparent in every page, but it is perhaps most pervasive and most important in discussions of the mysterious letter whose reappearances continually give us new hope that we will decode its meaning this time around, then frustrate that hope with new complexities or uncertainties.

When Joyce chose the title "Work in Progress" for the serialized segments of *Finnegans Wake*, he chose carefully, for the title refers not only to the incomplete state of the text in the period between 1923 and 1939, but also, and more importantly, to the "finished" text which constantly gives its readers the feeling that they are looking at something that is incomplete in itself—something that never permits any genuine resolution of the questions it raises but merely poses them in new, more enigmatic ways.[9] By concluding his book in the middle of a sentence, Joyce achieved the perfectly circular form he aimed at; but books are not printed in circular patterns, so the reader inevitably comes to the *end* and discovers that something is missing: an article like "the" makes little sense without a noun to modify, and unless we return to the opening page we are left hanging. The same pattern confronts the examiners of the letter which is supposed to have been written by Shem at the request of ALP, and is dug out of a dungheap by Biddy the Hen: the text of the letter is variously described as blurred, stained, punctured, incomplete, unsigned, indecipherable, untitled, and contradictory, while the envelope was apparently addressed to a nonexistent person and was "Opened by Miss Take" (*FW* 420.26). Thus, the failure to deliver the letter provides us with one more image of fragmentation or incompleteness, the unsuccessful odyssey of the letter being a metaphor for the reader's inability ever to reach a point where all the book's mysteries are revealed to him.

Although Joyce claimed to be able to communicate whatever he liked with language, he also recognized that the complexity of life requires that any such idea must be played off against its opposite, the counterpoint serving to indicate the futility of the search for absolute truth in a universe ruled by relativism, randomness, and uncertainty. Thus every time we encounter the letter, it has changed, which is another way of saying that in one sense, the letter is a work constantly in progress. Sometimes the epistle is sympathetic to Earwicker, sometimes it is hostile to him, and on occasion it seems to have nothing at all to do with him. Our first glimpse of the letter (*FW* 10–11) reveals nothing particularly suspicious, although on later examination we might recognize references to the two girls and three soldiers involved in Earwicker's sin in Phoenix Park ("Our pigeons pair are flewn for northcliffs. The three of crows have flapped it southenly"); most of the letter deals with the mother's role as preserver and restorer, a role reproduced in the act of digging the letter out of the dungheap so that later we can be told that "at this deleteful hour of dungflies dawning" we should be happy to have any letter to read, regardless of its condition (*FW* 118.31–34).

That the hen is on some level identified with the mother-wife figure, Anna Livia, becomes particularly evident in the fifth chapter, where Joyce devotes himself to an apparently exhaustive analysis of the letter from every possible angle. Here the hen who scratches the letter up from the midden heap becomes the wife as author of a letter in defense of her erring husband:

Mesdaims, Marmouselles, Mescerfs! Silvapais! All schwants (schwrites) ischt tell the cock's trootabout him. Kapak kapuk. No minzies matter. He had to see life foully the plak and the smut, (schwrites). There were three men in him (schwrites). Dancings (schwrites) was his only ttoo feebles. With apple harlottes. And a little mollvogels. Spissially (schwrites) when they peaches. Honeys wore camelia paints. Yours very truthful. Add dapple inn. (*FW* 113.11–18)

Several fundamental reading problems are illustrated by this passage. Many readers will catch echoes of familiar languages, including French (*Mesdames, mesdemoiselles, messieurs, s'il vous plaît*; *honi soit qui mal y pense*) and Latin (*camilla*: "maiden unblemished in birth and character"),[10] but without a reference guide few readers will catch puns on Albanian *kapak kapak* (little by little), *minzë* (pupil of eye), *plak* (old), *smût* (sick), *molle* (apple), or *vogel* (small).[11] Even a reading that includes all likely foreign language puns, all literary, geographical, and historical references, and everything else that we can imagine annotating, will not necessarily account for the relationship of these elements to one another or for the tone of the passage, so that even "that ideal reader suffering from an ideal insomnia" (*FW* 120.13–14) can never claim to have exhausted the possibilities of any given passage.

What appears at first to be the reader's real problem—the difficult language of the *Wake*, with its arcane references and multilingual puns—is actually more susceptible to remedy than the enduring dilemma of deciding what to do with the facts that we have marshalled. Again and again, the experience of *Wake* explicators is *not* that all the facts somehow reinforce one another and fit into a nice, easily summarized pattern, but, rather, that no general scheme accounts for all the elements in the text. This effect is quite intentional, and it is one of the book's real strengths; as Norman Rabkin has observed (writing of Shakespeare's plays), "If one hallmark of an authentic work of art and a central source of its power is its ability to drive us to search out its central mystery, another way may be its ultimate irreducibility to a schema."[12] *Finnegans Wake* constantly frustrates the move toward reductive interpretation, yet by throwing together great masses of materials that cannot always be reconciled with one another, Joyce imposes conditions on his reader that make impossible any reading that is not selective and reductive.[13] Reading *Finnegans Wake* thus becomes "a warping process" (*FW* 497.3), and those who have been victimized by the book's conflicting demands—that we select in order to systematize, and that we then recognize the inadequacy of our system—may well begin to regard themselves as martyrs.

The problem facing the reader may be defined in another way. As Manfred Pütz has observed, the fictitious reader of the *Wake* is only vaguely defined, and at times the reader is indistinguishable from the writer. Indeed, it appears that "Somebody (author) has written a letter to his other self (reader), penning it really to himself."[14] Part of the reason for this tendency of the reader and writer to blend into one another is that they both represent aspects of the dreamer, whose mind censors its own messages in order to prevent the guilty truth from being known. Margot Norris is therefore quite correct in analyzing the reader's situation in Freudian terms:

The great problem, of course, is that the reader is trapped inside the dream in *Finnegans Wake*. A dream can't be analyzed from the inside, because the dream is precisely the place where self-knowledge breaks down. The dreamer confronts a disguised message from his own unconscious. He is unable to know his unconscious directly, and yet it is utterly and truly himself. The confusion of the reader of *Finnegans Wake* is a fitting response to a kind of terror implicit in the world of the dream, a terror confronted by Alice in *Through the Looking-Glass* when Tweedledee suggests that she is merely a sort of thing in the Red Knight's dream.[15]

If the impossibility of ever fully understanding the message sent by the dreamer is one fundamental aspect of the reader's dilemma, a second aspect is the tantalizing effect of each new discovery, which leads us further into the search for ultimate meanings. The situation facing Joyce's readers is remarkably like the problem facing the inhabitants of the space station in Stanislaw Lem's science fiction novel

Solaris: hoping for contact with the planet Solaris, they are confronted again and again only with images of themselves and their own inability to understand the alien mind of the planet; yet no matter what happens to shatter their illusions they find themselves persisting "in the faith that the time of cruel miracles [is] not past." [16]

Similar problems appear to have beset Joyce himself as he composed *Finnegans Wake*, for at times he obviously intended his readers to see his meaning while at other times he stated that the book did not really have a meaning, at least not one that could be formulated in ordinary language. Atherton tells us that "Joyce considered that some knowledge of *The Book of the Dead* was necessary if *Finnegans Wake* was to be understood." [17] Joyce's own belief that the book could be "understood" is implied in such statements as his declaration to Armand Petitjean, "Why . . . you've nearly understood me," [18] or his complaint, "But I wish [Brancusi] or Antheil, say, could or would be as explicit as I try to be when people ask me: And what's this here, Guvnor?" (*L* I, 279). The opposite attitude is evident elsewhere, for example in his assertion that the book contains no "levels of meaning to be explored" but consists only of music and is intended to create laughter. [19] Caught between a desperate desire to be understood and widely read and a need to work with materials that would almost certainly limit his audience to a few polylingual insomniacs possessed either of a masochistic streak or a rich sense of their own absurdity, Joyce found the problems that would face his readers almost as burdensome as the readers themselves do. Thus, nearing the end of *Finnegans Wake*, we hear Joyce's own frustration emerging through Anna Livia's famous complaint: "A hundred cares, a tithe of troubles and is there one who understands me? One in a thousand of years of the nights?" (*FW* 627.14–16).

Despite the loneliness and alienation implied in this lament, Joyce and his reader are ultimately partners, not antagonists. If the reader cannot hope to understand exactly what Joyce meant when he wrote the book, it is equally true that the book lives only in the experience of its readers and has no set meaning apart from that experience. Although he makes many demands of his readers, Joyce accords them a place of honor in keeping with Sterne's dictum that "The truest respect which you can pay to the reader's understanding, is to halve this matter [of creating the book's meaning] amicably, and leave him something to imagine, as well as yourself." [20] Precisely so: and it is this reliance on the reader's cooperation (not to mention his good will, knowledge, sense of humor, patience, and insomnia) that defines Joyce's attitude toward his audience more accurately than the disdain of Professor Jones for his "muddlecrass pupils" (FW 152.8) or the absurdly reductive reading of the letter that boils it all down to a neat political allegory: "for we also know . . . that Father Michael about this red time of the white terror equals the old regime and Margaret is the social revolution while cakes mean the party funds and dear thank you signifies national gratitude" (FW 116.5–10). Much like the artist figure, Shem, the reader is treated ironically: he is a buffoon, a coward, a forger, or, echoing Baudelaire's address to his poor reader, "my shemblable! My freer!" (FW 489.28); yet he is also a hero, a sensitive figure with "a touch of the artist" about him, like Bloom. Treating his reader as an equal, Joyce invites him to join in his "grand funferall" (FW 13.15). The cover charge might at first seem steep, but many readers have discovered that the investment of their time and mental energy in following Joyce's "meanderthalltale" (FW 19.25) pays more than ample rewards. [21]

Notes

1. Hermione de Almeida, *Byron and Joyce through Homer: Don Juan and* Ulysses (New York: Columbia Univ. Pr., 1981), pp. 142–43.

2. Richard Ellmann, *James Joyce* (New York: Oxford Univ. Pr., 1959), p. 566.

3. Laurence Sterne, *The Life and Opinions of Tristram Shandy, Gentleman*, ed. James Aiken Work (New York: Odyssey, 1940), p. 73.

4. Sterne, p. 56.

5. C. S. Lewis, *A Preface to* Paradise Lost (London: Oxford Univ. Pr., 1942), p. 1.

6. Sheldon R. Brivic, *Joyce between Freud and Jung* (Port Washington, N.Y.: Kennikat, 1980), pp. 199–200.

7. Umberto Eco, *The Role of the Reader: Explorations in the Semiotics of Texts*

(Bloomington: Indiana Univ. Pr., 1979), p. 3. Elsewhere in the same volume, Eco remarks that "the work of James Joyce is a major example of an 'open' mode, since it deliberately seeks to offer an image of the ontological and existential situation of the contemporary world" (p. 54). In fact, the *Wake* approaches Roland Barthes' ideal of the "writerly text": "a perpetual present, upon which no *consequent* language (which would inevitably make it past) can be superimposed; the writerly text is *ourselves writing*, before the infinite play of the world (the world as function) is traversed, intersected, stopped, plasticized by some singular system (Ideology, Genus, Criticism) which reduces the plurality of entrances, the opening of networks, the infinity of languages"—*S/Z*, trans. Richard Miller (New York: Hill and Wang, 1974), p. 5. Cf. Jonathan Culler's comments about the *Wake* in *Structuralist Poetics: Structuralism, Linguistics and the Study of Literature* (Ithaca: Cornell Univ. Pr., 1975), p. 230.

8. Wolfgang Iser, *The Implied Reader: Patterns of Communication in Prose Fiction from Bunyan to Beckett*, trans. D. H. Wilson (Baltimore: Johns Hopkins Univ. Pr., 1974), p. 175.

9. Typically, Joyce often includes his provisional title in the text, to indicate that his work is still "in progress"—e.g., in "Work your progress!" (*FW* 473.21; cf. 465.8 [wip], 567.20, 609.31, 614.31, 625.13–14). The pattern is carried one step further when he alludes to the commentary on "Work in Progress" in the twelve *Exagmination* articles—"the contonuation through regeneration of the urutteration of the word in pregross" (*FW* 284.20–22); "Your exagmination round his factification for incamination of a warping process" (*FW* 497.2–3). It is interesting that Eco (*The Role of the Reader*, p. 56) uses a similar term, "works in movement," for a special type of open work that contains "unplanned or physically incomplete structural units"; although the idea that parts of *Finnegans Wake* were genuinely unplanned has surely been laid to rest, everything about the book is intended to suggest randomness and incompleteness in design.

10. Brendan O Hehir and John Dillon, *A Classical Lexicon for* Finnegans Wake (Berkeley: Univ. of California Pr., 1977), p. 79.

11. Roland McHugh, *Annotations to* Finnegans Wake (Baltimore: Johns Hopkins Univ. Pr., 1980), p. 113.

12. Norman Rabkin, *Shakespeare and the Problem of Meaning* (Chicago: Univ. of Chicago Pr., 1981), p. 23.

13. The same fundamental problem confronts the reader of *Ulysses*; cf. Iser, p. 226.

14. Manfred Pütz, "The Identity of the Reader in *Finnegans Wake*," *James Joyce Quarterly*, 11 (1974), 389.

15. Margot Norris, *The Decentered Universe of* Finnegans Wake (Baltimore: Johns Hopkins Univ. Pr., 1976), p. 78.

16. Stanislaw Lem, *Solaris*, trans. Joanna Kilmartin and Steve Cox (New York: Walker, 1970), p. 204.

17. James S. Atherton, *The Books at the Wake* (New York: Viking, 1960), p. 192. Atherton's next comment is revealing: "It is unfortunate that Joyce never explained why this [knowledge] was necessary."

18. Ellmann, p. 683n.

19. Ellmann, pp. 715–16.

20. Sterne, p. 109.

21. This essay is itself a work in progress, for it outlines ideas that I plan to develop at greater length in a reader-response analysis of *Ulysses* and *Finnegans Wake*. For several invaluable suggestions at this stage I wish to thank my colleague Steven Mailloux.

5

EDMUND L. EPSTEIN

James Joyce and Language

In Joyce's most recent work, *Finnegans Wake*, the destruction of language is completed.[1]

It should go without saying, at this centennial point, that James Joyce was both the master of the English language and, as an Irishman, the servant of it. Indeed, since language is usually the servant of thought, he was the server of a servant. "My soul frets in the shadow of his language" (*P* 189) thinks Stephen Dedalus, resisting the snares of the English dean of studies. Studying Joyce, we find our souls fretting, in the musical sense, in the shadow of his language.

Could anything new be said of Joyce's language, after Hugh Kenner and Anthony Burgess? Literary analysis by the means of modern linguistics finds its greatest challenge in Joyce, the greatest master of the English language since Milton, according to another practitioner.

Joyce was conscious of his control of English and other languages. He could do anything with language, he declared. He did more things with it than anyone who readily springs to mind. Yet his experiments are widespread; some are still undiscovered.

He is highly experimental in *Dubliners* in several places. Joyce gives us the clue to his linguistic heterodoxy on the very first page of "The Sisters," with the young boy hypnotized by the sounds of *pa-*

ralysis, gnomon, simony. At least two of these words are derived from Greek. Was Joyce even in 1903 searching for Odysseus? Homer himself is a famous experimenter in language, so much so that literary criticism, grammar, and linguistic criticism of verbal artifacts all trace their origin to the early scholiasts on Homer. Joyce's own *drang nach Osten* begins to drag him eastward very soon.

In addition, the hypnotic effect of the words themselves, apart from any meaning they might have, provides a focus on the verbal signifier, which eventually intensifies into a partial identification of the sign with the signified in *Finnegans Wake*, as we will see. In *Dubliners*, however, the usage is not really ever innocent. Joyce limits himself, by Kenner's "Uncle Charles principle," to fiction and syntax appropriate to the characters. By this principle, the text reads sometimes as if the characters themselves were writing it, as if Joyce had lent them his pen. However, some parts of *Dubliners* possess a linguistic subtlety, a treachery, almost, of surface that shows a creator aiding his creatures to express themselves. (After all, the father-figure in the Willingdone Museyroom tenders his matchbox to his tumescent and furious son to light a bomb with [*FW* 11]!) Consider for example the oddity of the following sentence from "An Encounter": "This rebuke during the sober hours of school paled much of the glory of the Wild West for me and the confused puffy face of Leo Dillon awakened one of my consciences" (*D* 20).

"One of my consciences"? How many consciences does a boy possess? Could Joyce (not the protagonist of "An Encounter") be using the word in one of its French senses of "consciousness"? If so, Joyce would be using the word in its root sense of "inward knowledge," or "inwit," as he later glosses it in *Ulysses*. "Conscience" would represent any awareness of inner mental reality, among which may be counted interior monologue, emotional upsurges, and public symbolic landscapes.

It is odd that conscience in the sense of inner knowledge, inwit, is a word with a treacherous surface, because Joyce also uses "remorse" in a "root" sense, in a "A Little Cloud": "Little Chandler felt his cheeks suffused with shame and he stood back out of the lamplight. He listened while the paroxysm of the child's sobbing grew less and less; and tears of remorse started to his eyes" (D 85).

"Remorse" seems oddly chosen. Little Chandler may feel sorry that he shouted at his baby, but the "remorse" is aroused more by his fright at his wife's vehemence than by any actual movement of conscience toward the amendment of bad action. His "remorse" is much more than a feeling that he has been a bad boy for shouting at his son; he is mourning for his lost youth. In fact, he is one of those Joycean fathers who has not yet accepted his role as father because of immaturity, like Farrington of "Counterparts." Farrington is treated roughly by his society, and in turn he beats his own son, as he has been "punished" by his society. Counterparts, indeed! Both Little Chandler and Farrington have become paralyzed between youth and maturity and cannot be fathers in spirit. This spiritual imbalance exacerbates their tempers, but whereas Farrington passes on the beating he has received, Little Chandler weeps like his own child. "Remorse" is not here the indispensable canonical requirement for absolution; it is sterile mental distress, the bite of the worm of "conscience," inner knowledge, in Hell. "Remorse" is, therefore, "agenbite," by what linguists call a "calque," a rendering syllable by syllable of a word in one language into another. "Inwit" is also a calque: con = in: scientia = knowledge = wit. Just so does re = agen; mordere, morsus = bite. Remorse of conscience is a biting of inward knowledge, whether leading to repentance or not. Stephen's "remorse" in *Ulysses* does not lead him to repent. His "remorse" is an inward biting of the mind, an almost physical gnawing away of his morale: "Agenbite of inwit. Inwit's agenbite. Misery! Misery!" (U 243). It is this internal "biting" that causes tears of pain to rise to the eyes of the paralyzed, doomed Little Chandler. "Remorse," taken in its usual meaning, seems to lack relevance, but in its root meaning it is all too pertinent.

Joyce is constantly aware of the "nest of evil in the bosom of a good word" (FW 189.29–30); this extension of significance is his own contribution to the text, otherwise "written" by his characters. "Incest" is buried in "insect"; "biting" is hidden in "remorse." Another term, "vanity" as employed in "Araby," is also transparent: "Gazing up into the darkness I saw myself as a creature driven and derided by vanity; and my eyes burned with anguish and anger" (*D* 35). Surely this is too extreme a reaction to disappointment. He may feel that his romantic dreams are immature, but what is more romantic than a darkened hall with flirtations taking place in the only lighted area? The mature Joyce would have felt this, but the shallow romanticism of the boy has been rudely rebuffed by the world. Yet why "vanity"? In its modern sense of "preening self-conceit" or "inordinate pride in one's own person or attainments" the word seems inappropriate. The boy is not proud of his body or of his attainments; at most he is possessed by a boyish chivalry, which is touching and appropriate rather than exaggerated and self-regarding. No: here "vanity" returns to its original meaning. It is derived from the Vulgate version of *Ecclesiastes*: *Vanitas vanitatum*, Jerome's rendering of the Hebrew *hevel havalim*. "Hevel" in Hebrew means "an exhalation, a breathing," or by extension mere breath rather than substance, emptiness rather than content. "Emptiness of emptiness" is how the preacher, Koheleth, or Ecclesiastes, judges all the facts of human life; "emptiness of emptiness" is the way Hebrew conveys "the most extreme emptiness"; Hebrew lacks a way to convey superlatives. ("Shira haShirim"—"The Song of Songs"—means "The Greatest Song"). *Vana* in Latin means *empty*, and so Jerome's *vanitas vanitatum* literally translates the Hebrew.

The next stop in the journey to Joyce's "vanity" is in the seventeenth century. Bunyan's "Vanity Fair" in *Pilgrim's Progress* means the fair where only emptiness is sold, but because Vanity Fair is a fair the term *vanity* has acquired a sense of a conscious clothing and adorning of the person. From that to the modern sense of "inordinate pride in one's personal attainments" is a short step. Joyce shows that he is aware of the history of the word, by the setting of the end of "Araby"—a fair in which nothing valuable is sold. The Araby bazaar is a Vanity Fair, in fact. The use of "vanity" is here part of a verbal mosaic which should coalesce with the phrase "Vanity Fair" in the mind of the reader, outside of awareness. "Empty Fair," the emptiness of the Dreams of Fair Women entertained by the boy, is the true significance of the last sections of the story.

The mature Joyce is not abashed by the "emptiness" of human life. Rather than encouraging in himself a spirit of *contemptus mundi*, which is the traditional attitude of the Church toward things of this world, Joyce dedicated himself and his powers to the portraying of the phenomenal world, poised and sustained upon the void. In the *Wake* his spokesman, St. Patrick, successfully defends the delusory rainbow of the visible-audible-gnosible world against the sage Koheleth or the Druid. The immaturity of the boy in "Araby" is shown by his "remorse" (if you will) upon contemplating the emptiness of his own Vanity Fair, an emptiness which will sustain the mature creation of Joyce. "Hell flies like a bubble before the breath of God," declares the *Faust-Book*. The whole universe is a bubble which Joyce portrays in his mere exhalations recorded on paper— *hevel havalim*—the acceptance of emptiness and the weaving together of its empty exhalations by a "weaver of the wind" (*U* 25). It might seem impossible to modulate Koheleth's mere breath into Joyce's sound-symbols of a world, but Joyce seems to have done it.

A Portrait contains many points of linguistic interest. One especially deserves comment. When Father Dolan erupts into Father Arnall's classroom, a linguistic ambiguity hastens disaster for Stephen. Father Dolan demands angrily why Stephen is not writing his lesson, and Father Arnall replies, "He broke his glasses . . . and I exempted him from work" (*P* 49). Father Dolan considers this "an old schoolboy trick" and pandies Stephen. Father Arnall does not intercede, perhaps obscurely influenced by the fear that the recent death of Parnell has brought on a spirit of rebellion that requires the repressing hand of temporary injustice to quell. Father Arnall's phrase is syntactically ambiguous, and Father Dolan can interpret it in the sense he wishes. "He broke his glasses" could bear what the linguists call an "ergative" interpretation. An ergative case for a noun or pronoun is appropriate whenever an actual action is performed (*erg-* being the Greek root for "work"). Therefore,

John kicked Bill.
Sam carved his name on a tree.
Stephen broke his glasses.

all represent action *deliberately undertaken* with a resultant alteration in the world. This is the interpretation that Father Dolan seizes, and which Father Arnall does not correct.

The intended meaning of the sentence is that the glasses became broken without ergative intention on the part of Stephen. Therefore, the sentence would resemble such apparently transitive but non-ergative sentences as *John loves Mary* (he is not performing a deliberate *action* upon her), or, *The wind scattered the grain* (this was the *effect* of the wind, not its deliberate *action*). In French the ergative interpretation would produce the sentence, *Il cassait ses lunettes*. The non-ergative intention might require some such phrase as *Il se cassait ses lunettes!* [2] English does not allow the clarity of French. It uses the same phrase to mean two things: "Stephen deliberately broke his glasses to avoid work," an old schoolboy trick, and not, as Father Arnell intended, "Stephen's glasses became broken by an accident." It is characteristic of Joyce to ascribe drastic results to subtle ambiguities in English syntax.

Ulysses contains so many examples of linguistic subtlety that a book could be written on the subject. In *Ulysses* Joyce locates the source of linguistic creativity in the deepest instinctual centers of the human mind. In the Circe episode, Lipoti Virag represents both the Freudian Id, the center of aggressive and libidinal drives, and the source of language. He wears a *pshent*, the Egyptian crown found on the head of Thoth, god of language, and bears two quills behind his ears like a secretary-bird. He is also "basilicogrammate," the bearer of the sovereign word. [3] Words and syllables pop out of him alarmingly, and his phrases are clotted with unassociated articles, personal, relative and possessive pronouns and demonstratives: "That the cows with their those distended udders that they have been the known. . ." (*U* 516). It is at this point that Joyce acknowledges the self-impelling power of language as a phenomenon in itself and not only as a mirror of reality. Language has its own momentum and its own rules of cohesion.

In *Ulysses* and *Finnegans Wake* language has its free play conceded to it, frequently to the distress of readers, who often cry out, in the words of the *Wake*, that the text is nothing but a pure and simple jangle of words (*FW* 112.4). Is anything in the *Wake* pure and simple? To answer my own rhetorical question, yes, the *Wake* is as simple as it can be, thus conforming to the principle of the economy of Nature's laws, as shaved by Occam's razor. Indeed, since the subject of the *Wake* is all of human life, one could almost argue that Joyce has oversimplified the subject matter; the *Wake* is much less confusing than life itself, any person's life. Joyce employs languages as a simplifying device, a filter through which passes only the essence of human life.

Any writer of the present age must wrestle with the chaotic nature of his subject matter. Matter was always seen as inchoate, but it is only in our age that the chaos was a matter of principle. Samuel Beckett declared that a new form in art will be necessary to deal with the chaos: "this form will be of such a type that it admits the chaos and does not try to say that the chaos is really something else. . . . To find a form that accommodates the mess, that is the task of the artist now."[4] Joyce created a form with his "hyperpoems," long stretches of apparent prose, incorporating a great miscellany of material-scientific facts, business forms, tide-tables, hesitations, exclamations, but which is nevertheless poetry. It is as if the Liffey, along with the garbage it bears on its surface, were regarded as a concrete hyperpoem. The Ithaca chapter of Ulysses contains many such hyperpoems, the most impressive sequence of which occurs on the subject of water:

What in water did Bloom, waterlover, drawer of water, watercarrier returning to the range, admire?
Its universality: its democratic equality and constancy to its nature in seeking its own level: its vastness in the ocean of Mercator's projection: its

unplumbed profundity in the Sundam trench of the Pacific exceeding 8,000 fathoms: the restlessness of its waves and surface particles visiting in turn all points of its seaboard: the independence of its units: the variability of states of sea: its hydrostatic quiescence in calm: its hydrokinetic turgidity in neap and spring tides: its subsidence after devastation: its sterility in the circumpolar icecaps, arctic and antarctic: its climatic and commercial significance: its preponderance of 3 to 1 over the dry land of the globe: its indisputable hegemony extending in square leagues over all the region below the subequatorial tropic of Capricorn: the multisecular stability of its primeval basin: its luteofulvous bed: its capacity to dissolve and hold in solution all soluble substances including millions of tons of the most precious metals: its slow erosions of peninsulas and downwardtending promontories: its alluvial deposits: its weight and volume and density: its imperturbability in lagoons and highland tarns. . . . (U 671–72)

Interspersed with the scientific prose we see poetry burning its way through, and the hyperpoem ends with a frankly acknowledged poeticism: "the noxiousness of its effluvia in lacustrine marshes, pestilential fens, faded flowerwater, stagnant pools in the waning moon" (U 672). It is as if Joyce had given himself permission to use any type of language in his search for exact expression, even the humblest.

Joyce could indeed do anything with language. It has been the experience of many *Wake* readers that the text seems to clear itself up; from the first chapters to the last the *Wake* becomes easier to read. Is it only that the reader becomes accustomed to Joyce's languages, "Djoytsch" or "Shemese," with experience? This may be part of the truth, but I think that Joyce may actually have succeeded in modulating his puns from obscure to clear from Book II to Book IV, as an iconic modelling of his diction on the principle of dark to light, as the *Wake* proceeds from dusk to midnight to dawn. It seems to me that Joyce deploys two grades of puns in the *Wake*, which rhetoricians would identify as *paronomasia* and *antanaclasis*. The difference between paronomasia and antanaclasis is that paronomasiac structures combine two words into a third which bears resemblances to both, but is itself a new creation; antanaclastic structures employ words that mean two different things without a wrenching awry of the word itself. Therefore, Joyce's "fairlygo-smother-" (*FW* 353.27) combines "fairly go smother" and "fairy-godmother." The two opposed meanings are those of suicide and magical transformation, for a paronomasiac creation. The "ab-nihilisation of the etym" (*FW* 353.22) destroys everything with annihilation of the atom, in Joyce's astonishing prediction of the atomic bomb, and the bringing about of creation from nothing (*ab nihil*) by the word creates everything anew.

As the *Wake* climbs out of midnight and moves towards dawn, the puns begin to clear, to move from paronomasia to antanaclasis. Even the paragraph which announces the first ante-lucan sifting of sunlight into the night of the *Wake* shows a movement from complexity to simplicity. Most of the paragraph is in perfectly clear English, with only an occasional paronomasia.

The phaynix rose a sun before Erebia sank his smother! Shoot up on that, bright Bennu Bird! *Va faotre!* Eftsoon so too will our own sphoenix spark spirt his spyre and sunward stride the rampante flambe. Ay, already the sombrer opacities of the gloom are sphanished! Brave footsore Haun! Work your progress! Hold to! Now! Win out, ye divil ye! The silent cock shall crow at last. The west shall shake the east awake. Walk while ye have the night for morn, lightbreakfastbringer, morroweth wheron every past shall full fost sleep. Amain. (*FW* 473.16–25)

This passage heralds the dawn, which at this point in the book (Book III.ii) is rising in eastern Spain ("sphoenix, sphanished") but sending signals ahead to Dublin five hundred miles to the west. The passage is for the most part in standard English, with a Dublin accent. There are a few paronomasias. "Erebia" equals *Arabia*, the habitat of the phoenix, "the Arabian bird" (Shakespeare), with *Erebus*, the dark underworld of the Greeks (perhaps from Semitic/Hebrew *yerev*, darkness.) The compound *Erebia* would contain both light and darkness.

"Smother" equals *mother* and *smotherer*. There are references to Verdi's *Il Trovatore* in the paragraph. "Stride the rampante flambe" contains a reference to the gypsy Azucena's aria "Stride la Vampa," in which she sings of her horror at her mother's execution by fire by the father of the Count di Luna, and of her kidnapping of the Count's son, the brother of the present count. Azucena attempted to kill the Count's son by throwing the baby into a fire, but found that she had killed her own baby by mistake, since which time she has raised the Count's brother as her own son. When the child, now the troubadour Manrico, is executed by the Count, she reveals to him that Manrico was his brother. The reference in the *Wake* combines the fires of Azucena's mother's pyre and the fire in which Azucena destroyed her own baby, which made her a "smother" in Joyce's system, and the Phoenix fire of the rising sun. "Haun" combines *Hahn*, German for "rooster," and *haunt*, the shade that Shaun is becoming—from Shaun to Jaun to Haun to Yawn.

These are the main paronomasias in the passage, but the effect of the paragraph depends upon antanaclases. The most important antanaclasis is, of course, son/sun. Osiris, torn to pieces by his brother Set, rises up as his own son/sun Horus in the Egyptian version of the sun-cycle. The pun survives only in English. Also "lightbreakfastbringer" is antanaclastic—the bringer of a light breakfast, on Sunday morning, and the bringer of light breaking forth on the sunrise.

The antanaclases cluster thicker and thicker, leading eventually to two of Anna Livia's phrases. In "How glad you'll be I waked you!" (*FW* 625.33), "wake" is, of course, the antanaclasis for the whole giant book, with two of its well-known meanings expressing opposites: "wake" as the watch over the dead, and "wake" as "arise." There is a third meaning, however, which is not so well known. The wake of a ship is important structurally in the *Wake*. Three of the books end with a river flowing outward—Book I (Anna Livia), Book II (the ship with the Four Old Men), and Book IV (Anna Livia's departure). The Prankquean Fable gives the clues to this wake; the family structure established at the end of the Fable combines the ship, the wave, and the wind: "The prankquean was to hold her dummyship and the jimminies was to keep the peacewave and van

Hoother was to git the wind up" (*FW* 23.12–14). The family ship sails out to sea into the sunrise, leaving a wake behind, which is the book we read. The title of *Finnegans Wake* is an antanaclasis.

The ending of Anna Livia's monologue and the ending of the book approach perfect clarity through antanaclasis. "I done me best when I was let. Thinking always if I go all goes" (*FW* 627.13–14). "Let" means both "allowed" and "hindered" (the archaic "let"). If the river is allowed to run it will do its best, but if it is hindered (as by hydroelectric schemes) it will also do its best. "If I go" means both "if I continue" and "if I die." Joyce even achieves an antanaclastic triumph with an omitted word: "My people were not their sort out beyond there so far as I can" (*FW* 627.24–25). See/sea is omitted because she cannot see well—her sight is failing as she dies. Yet she is gazing out to sea, which provides a stronger rhythm for her dying efforts.

The ending of the book is a technical triumph of language unapproached in modern literature. All the devices of poetry appear in Anna's *Liebestod*. The sounds of "bold," "bad," "bleary" (*FW* 627.25–26) are repeated in "And it's old and old it's sad and old it's sad and weary I go back to you, my cold father, my cold mad father, my cold mad feary father . . ." (*FW* 627.36–628.1–2). They are also echoed in the rhythm of "they'll never *see*. Nor *know*. Nor *miss me*" (*FW* 627.35–36; italics mine).

The actual ending of the book is a "bitter ending" in which the fresh water mingles with the bitter-salty water of the sea. Yet the rhythms are hypnotic, even traditional. Listen to the rhythm of the last sentence: "A way a lone a last a loved a long the" (*FW* 628.15–16). Here we have a perfect iambic pentameter line, with a feminine ending: ˘ - ˘ ˘ - ˘ - ˘ - ˘. The rhythm actually continues over to the first page again. If the last sentence is connected to the first, an iambic rhythm persists until Howth Castle is sighted: "Ă wāy ă lōne ă lāst ă lōved ă lōng thĕ rīvĕrrūn, păst Ēve ănd Ādăms, frŏm swērve ŏf shōre tŏ bēnd ŏf bāy" (*FW* 628.15–16, 3.1–2). The rhythm is broken only at "from," with its extra weak stress, another feminine ending. Then the businesslike male rhythms begin, with "brings us by a commodius vicus of recirculation back to Howth Castle and Environs."

The syntax of the last/first sentence is extremely odd. The last sentence, with "riverrun," seems to bear the meaning, "Away, alone at last, and loved, along the river ran"; that is, Anna Livia is running "away" from the land, and is "alone at last," since "delth" has parted her from her husband and family; however, she is "loved" by the sea, which is mixed with her and bears her up and backwards, as the tide turns. So "along the river ran," to caverns measureless to man. However, the syntax of this sentence—an intransitive construction preceded by adjectival oppositives—will not fit the syntax of the rest of the sentence: "riverrun . . . brings us to Howth Castle and Environs." This sentence is transitive, with "us" the object. Joyce has fused an intransitive sentence with a transitive one: "along the river ran," with "the river-run brings us to Howth Castle and Environs."

Perhaps Joyce is conveying the turn of the tide, the *sandhi* between death and life by his mixed form. Anna Livia feels the kiss which gives her the keys to life; then she flows away in language to the beginning of life again.

Notes

1. Ernst Robert Curtius, "James Joyce and His Ulysses," *Essays on European Literature*, trans. Michael Kowal (Princeton: Princeton Univ. Pr., 1973), p. 355.

2. The English of this might be some such odd phrase as *He got himself a broken pair of glasses* (by carelessness).

3. I treat this subject in greater detail in *A Starchamber Quiry*, ed. E. L. Epstein (London: Methuen, 1982).

4. Statement by Beckett to Tom F. Driver, "Beckett by the Madeleine," *Columbia University Forum* 4, No. 3 (1961), p. 23.

6

MARGARET CHURCH

Time as an Organizing Principle in the Fiction of James Joyce

Perhaps the most important pioneer work on the structural significance of time in the fiction of James Joyce was done by William York Tindall in *James Joyce: His Way of Interpreting the Modern World*.[1] Here Tindall argued that "to replace Christianity Joyce needed a system in which man could occupy the center" and that in effecting this, "cyclical recurrence became his substitute for metaphysics."[2] However, Tindall accords only two paragraphs to cyclical patterns in *A Portrait* and *Ulysses*, and his main discussion of the topic centers on *Finnegans Wake*, to which he devotes the majority of the chapter called "Family Cycle."

Although Tindall offers a rich perspective on Joyce's possible sources for cyclical recurrence (among them Plato, Vergil, Shelley, Jung, and Yeats), probably the most convincing case is made for Giambattista Vico, whose philosophy of history is explained in his *La Scienza nuova* (1725). Tindall makes it plain that Joyce preferred Vico to other "cyclists," and he demonstrates this by describing the three Viconian Ages and the reflux that appear in each of the four books of *Finnegans Wake*, the main structure being a large cycle containing four smaller ones, as well as many other wheels within wheels. Such juxtaposition of cycles within cycles provides complex levels of meaning: contrasts and contraries made to compare and to run parallel; antitheses uniting. Joyce turned to both Nicholas of Cusa and to Giordano Bruno of Nola for the theory of the "coincidence of contraries," which involves the unity of the cycle, "each thing is the starting point of its contrary,"[3] a theory discovered also in the work of Hegel.

In the same chapter Tindall proceeds to a discussion of the influence of Bishop Berkeley, "the subjective idealist"; of J. W. Dunne and his concept of serial time; and of Eddington and the expanding universe. Joyce found eternity, according to Tindall, in "the historical pattern, the family and man," rather than in the "absolute time" of Bergson and of Proust.[4]

In 1950 Tindall opened a veritable cache of critical subject matter for scholars who followed him. In reviewing Tindall's work, Richard Kain writes: "If the initiate suffer at times a certain headiness from finding symbol within symbol and cycle within cycle, he cannot deny that such correspondences were among Joyce's constant preoccupations."[5] In 1951, A. M. Klein elaborated on Vico's influence in the Nestor episode of *Ulysses*,[6] and in 1956 Fred H. Higginson explored a sentence in *Finnegans Wake* suggesting Quinet, Vico, and Bruno as fundamental keys to the book.[7]

The 1950s were also to see important discussions and exegeses of the stream of consciousness technique (stemming from a Bergsonian base) as well as Shiv K. Kumar's early work on space-time polarity in *Finnegans Wake*.[8] Citing, like Tindall, both Nicholas of Cusa and Bruno of Nola, Kumar points out that "the contrapuntal nature of space and time"[9] is symbolized by both character and episode in *Finnegans Wake*. Shem symbolizes duration; Shaun is space-oriented. Direct allusions to the space-time polarity which undergirds the structure of *Finnegans Wake* are also numerous, riverrun circulating and recirculating throughout and within and around the environs of the city of Dublin.

However, the works of Robert Humphrey, Hans Meyerhoff, and Melvin Friedman must be seen as the central discussions of stream of consciousness in the decade of the 50s.[10] Humphrey, dealing with *Ulysses*, points out that the formless nature of the psychic life of his characters forced Joyce to impose exterior patterns on his narrative; thus, rigid form and formlessness interact in creating the effect of the novel. One pattern is, of course, the eighteen hours of one day;

another is one city and its geography. A third device is the use of motif, such as the image of Stephen's dying mother or Bloom's potato. The burlesque or parody of Homer's *Odyssey* is still another deliberate attempt to create a form that will offset and add meaning to the free-flowing processes of consciousness. Similarly, Meyerhoff pointed out how Joyce injects into the stream of consciousness the hours of the day. The unities of time, self, and narrative are thus rendered: "time and life form a unity within the most bewildering multiplicity."[11] Meyerhoff is one of the first critics to suggest that the cyclical theory of Vico may have had significant impact on Joyce's fiction as early as *A Portrait*, enabling Joyce to rediscover the mythical Daedalus at the book's end.[12] Melvin Friedman's more extensive treatment of the stream of consciousness technique explores its backgrounds, mentioning in some detail William James, Bergson, Freud, Jung, Larbaud, and Dujardin, the last of whom Joyce referred to as the source of his own interior monologue. Friedman maintains that Joyce's fiction demonstrates the fullest development of the potential of the stream of consciousness method. Cadence, internal rhythm, fluidity, and balance reach perfection in the long monologue of Molly at the end of *Ulysses*.

Seven years later, in 1962, Shiv K. Kumar was to deal more narrowly with the influence of Bergson, T. E. Hulme, and William James on narrative technique in Joyce's work. Bergson's sense of fluid reality was a phenomenon of the *Zeitgeist*, according to Kumar, and he speaks thus of parallels rather than of influences. His chapter on Joyce, like Friedman's, serves to point out the role of flux, of a continuum, in the novels, a "conception of life as a river rushing on unimpeded."[13]

Time as an organizing principle was seen in still a different perspective by Robert Ryf in 1962 in his *A New Approach to Joyce*,[14] one of the most perceptive critical works on Joyce written in the 1960s. Ryf sees *A Portrait* as a nuclear work around which all the rest of Joyce's fiction revolves in expanding circles. Taken together, Joyce's canon tells one story: first, of those who do not escape the nets in *Dubliners*; of the microcosm of self that does escape in *A Portrait*; of

modern man coming to terms with the world in which he lives in
Ulysses; and finally of the circle of human history in *Finnegans Wake*.
"If the *Portrait* is the microcosm and *Ulysses* the cosmos, then *Finnegans Wake* is the macrocosm." [15] Such a pattern contains curious
and intriguing echoes of the Viconian system: *Dubliners* represents
the Age of the Fathers (Gods) from whom one may not escape; *Portrait*, the Age of the Sons (heroes), who rebel in order to escape and to
attain freedom of choice; *Ulysses*, the Age of the People, the world to
which Bloom and Stephen must adjust; and *Finnegans Wake*, the
ricorso ("fall if you will but rise you must"), [16] the fall of empire and
its regeneration in new forms. Thus, Ryf's pattern is essentially
temporal, suggesting the various ages of man as in the riddle of the
sphinx.

Thus far two major temporal patterns have emerged in critical
assessments of Joyce's works: a structured Viconian pattern and a
more freeflowing Bergsonian one, one socially and historically ori-
ented, the other individually. Joyce's own work tends to move in
constant tension between these two forces, the society of which each
Dubliner is a part and the individual citizen of that Dublin. My own
book *Time and Reality* (1963) dealt with both influences, though
stressing the Bergsonian. Along with the influence of Bergson, my
chapter on Joyce indicates the importance of Jung and Freud for
Joyce (despite his expressed preference for Dujardin) in developing
his sense of free association, the stream of consciousness, and the
recurrent myth. [17] My chapter traces as well the incipient influence of
Vico's ages of man in *Ulysses*, leaving the full impact of Vico for the
discussion of *Finnegans Wake*.

Interest in the relation between Vico and Joyce substantially esca-
lated after the early 1960s. In an article published in 1964, Matthew
Hodgart singles out a sentence near the end of the Cyclops episode
for analysis. [18] The sentence contains the name of "the right hon-
ourable sir Hercules Hannibal Habeas Corpus Anderson K.G.,
K.P. . . ," which according to Hodgart may reflect the three stages
of Viconian history: "Hercules (the age of the giants and theocracy);
Hannibal (the age of heroes and feudalism); and Habeas Corpus (the

age of law and democracy)."[19] Hodgart goes on to trace other Viconian motifs throughout the Cyclops chapter.

In 1969 A. Walton Litz's essay on Joyce and Vico appeared in Giorgio Tagliacozzo's symposium volume on Vico.[20] Litz attests to the undisputed power of Vico over Joyce's imagination, but claims no specific role for Vico in *Dubliners* or *Portrait*, only that "interest in heroic types and cyclic form"[21] which made Joyce so receptive to Vico. In *Ulysses*, however, Litz finds a "conscious intention" and an ambiguous role for Viconian views: "although Joyce clearly had Vico in mind, he did not demand that the reader share this association."[22] Litz sees Vico's chief influence in the structures of *Finnegans Wake*: "This four-part cycle, with its historical and personal implications, pervades every aspect of *Finnegans Wake*, governing the construction of words and sentences as well as the largest structural patterns."[23] Not only was Joyce influenced by Vico's cyclic view of history but by his treatment of language.

My 1968 article on *Dubliners* broke new ground in asserting that Vico could have been an important influence for Joyce as early as 1903 and in demonstrating a Viconian pattern in *Dubliners*.[24] The first three stories portray not only childhood but also an ironic image of Vico's first age, the Divine Age or Age of the Parents. The Heroic Age or Age of the Sons may be seen in the next eight stories, populated with sons reared by the kind of parents we meet in the first three tales. These are "anti-heroes" incapable of supplying the support and guidance they themselves have been denied. In Vico's Human Age, represented by the next three stories, we find that the committees and councils of this society are equally corrupt, and the final story, "The Dead," serves as the *ricorso*, representing the eternal dance of recirculation, the grouping and regrouping of human energies.

Likewise in 1976, my chapter "*Portrait* and Giambattista Vico: A Source Study" in *Approaches to Joyce's Portrait* established a clear Viconian pattern for that novel.[25] Vico's Divine Age may be seen as the basis of chapter one, where we view Stephen submissive to his parents and to the parent priests at Clongowes. In addition, the older boys at school provide models of mock divinity. The second chapter, where Uncle Charles is relegated to the outhouse and Stephen's mind turns to Mercedes and the Count of Monte Cristo, constitutes the Heroic Age. Hints of rivalry may be found in conversations between Simon Dedalus and his son, but at the end, Stephen's dreams of Mercedes are actualized in the arms of a prostitute. The Age of the People is seen in chapter three, where Stephen achieves, even though temporarily, uneasy religious communion with his fellow man. And the *ricorso* occurs in chapter four, where images of falling, of bridges crossed, of epiphany and prophecy prefigure a turning of the tide and the beginning of a new Viconian cycle. It is my contention that chapter five is a second Age of the Fathers in which the parents and priests of chapter one are replaced by the gods of the university, those who teach literature, art, and philosophy, and under whose authority Stephen now places himself. This Age of the Fathers leads into a new Heroic Age, the Age of Telemachus in the first chapter of *Ulysses*.

In 1978, my essay "Fiction: The Language of Time" (in *The Study of Time*) went on to trace this pattern in *Ulysses*, the first three chapters of which continue a cycle begun in the last chapter of *A Portrait*.[26] Telemachus suggests the Age of the Heroes, Nestor the Age of the People, and Proteus the *ricorso*, where the swirling waters of the sea metaphorically depict circulation and recirculation, like Proteus himself, an everchanging form. The twelve chapters of the middle section of *Ulysses* may be divided into three groupings of four and similarly interpreted. Thus in Calypso, Bloom is seen initially as a kind of mock *paterfamilias*; in the Lotus Eaters, engaged in narcissistic and titillating adolescent activity; in Hades, in a communal setting with friends and citizens of Dublin; and in Aeolus, at the newspaper offices, where circulation and recirculation characterize existence.

My essay traces similar arrangements in the next eight sections of *Ulysses*, arriving finally at the Nostos where the last three sections can be seen as the beginning of a new cycle that culminates in the giant *ricorso* of *Finnegans Wake* or "riverrun," the first word of that ever-cycling book. Joyce thereby links together his three central fictional works by means of Viconian cycles left to be completed in the succeeding novel. He uses Vico as a structural means to unify his entire canon, the course of history being seen as a recurrent building up, then breaking down of form (in the four *ricorsi*, Proteus, Aeolus, Sirens, Circe, of *Ulysses*). The wavelike structure of all process is thus represented in Joyce's narration of events on a June day in the city of Dublin.

The late 1960s and early 1970s were to see new and exciting reinterpretations and repudiations of Vico's influence on Joyce. In 1966 in an essay, *"Finnegans Wake* in Perspective," Clive Hart renounced his own earlier Viconian interpretation of *Finnegans Wake* through symphony, fable, nightmare, and macromyth ("The Viconian cycle of ages").[27] Rather than rationality, architecture, internal coherence, Hart now saw a "fractured and distorted surface," enabling the reader to lead the text where he might like. Consistency is achieved by linguistic phenomena, which, as Joyce himself said, should be allowed to affect us "as such."[28] Hart was thus one of the first critics to open the door to structuralist interpretations of *Finnegans Wake* which have resulted in such studies as Margot Norris's *The Decentered World of* Finnegans Wake: *A Structural Analysis.*[29]

In an essay published in 1974, Norris remarked that although Joyce valued Vico as a social historian, Vico failed to provide him "with an individual psychology to complement his social theories. . . ." The theories of Vico or Bruno of Nola are thus for Norris structural principles rather than the "models, plans or patterns" which I had outlined in my articles on this subject. For example, the four Viconian cycles enable us better to understand the relationships of fathers, sons, and brothers as they rise and fall in *Finnegans Wake*, but they provide no neat blueprint of the work.[30]

Likewise, in 1973 Patrick White claimed that there was no ontological or psychological justification for the use of Viconian cycles in *Ulysses*.[31] Attempts to discover such cycles (he cites, in a footnote, Mason, Tindall, Klein, Church) merely support the dubious notion that the order of *Ulysses* is "an imposed order,

a purely aesthetic order." "Instead of imposing one or more of
Vico's cycles on the action of the novel, Joyce locates the action at a
stationary point along Vico's ideal, eternal history that is traversed
in time by the actual history of all nations." This stationary point is
for White located within the *ricorso* or "period of disintegration" of
Vico. With this in mind White examines in some detail the Hades
episode and burial rites, concluding that what redeems contemporary man is that "he did not choose to be born into such a period of
disintegration."[32]

One of the most challenging treatments of Joyce and Vico in the
1970s was that of Stuart Hampshire in a 1973 review of Norman O.
Brown's *Closing Time*.[33] Hampshire takes pains to repudiate what he
sees as Brown's "literal and immediate interpretation of Vico." In
language almost as lyrical and literate as Joyce's, Hampshire points
to the larger focus on Vico to be found in Joyce's work: "the great
revolving years of ideal history"; "the renewals and returns and dis-
guises" that remove him from pessimism; the middle way between a
definition of human nature as unchanging and human nature as essentially "open to development without limit." "Humanity," writes
Hampshire, "ascends or descends only as day into night, or spring
into winter, in the long cadence which allows one leading nation or
leading family or leading hero to succeed another in the returning
and renewing circle of spiritual seasons."[34]

Treatments of stream of consciousness technique in Joyce also
continued in the 1970s. Richard Peterson pointed out in 1973 that
Dubliners, in which Joyce depicts "the paralyzing and destructive
effect of time," may have been the spur which encouraged him to lay
emphasis on "human time and timelessness" in the fiction that followed it.[35] In 1971 K. E. Robinson explored psychological time in
A Portrait, breaking the book into two structural units of stream of
consciousness, one interior, the other narrated and beginning after
the asterisk in chapter four.[36]

The most extensive treatment of stream of consciousness in the
1970s is Erwin Steinberg's *The Stream of Consciousness and Beyond in
Ulysses* for which there is not space in this essay for a detailed re-

view.[37] Steinberg examines the psychological stream of consciousness and its relationship to language, Joyce's use of the technique, the extent to which he reproduces it, and how it is employed in the opening chapters of *Ulysses*. Part two of Steinberg's book compares the streams of consciousness of Stephen, Bloom, and Molly and how they shape the idiosyncrasies of character in the book, thus developing a new tool for the novelist and resolving disagreements about meaning. In part three Steinberg discusses the development of Joyce's prose style and tries to account for his interest in the technique of the stream of consciousness as he moved beyond it "to the polyphonic technique of *Finnegans Wake*."[38]

Present interest in temporal patterns of organization in Joyce's work continues to center on structures already discussed in this essay and to open still further avenues of approach to the subject. Among new approaches is Hugh Kenner's recent guide to *Ulysses*.[39] Rather than offering a durational or patterned structure, Kenner concentrates on the tapestry that exists outside of time, pieces of which weave in and out of the pages of the book. Kenner reassembles symbol and motif so that new elements in *Ulysses* become apparent, thus establishing a supra-temporal structure as its base. Another new study, that of Craig Wallace Barrow, elaborates on a cinematographic perspective on *Ulysses*.[40] Barrow points out that montage, both primary and simultaneous, serves an important function in the interior monologue of the book, which he proceeds to analyze chapter by chapter. In *The Transformation Process in Joyce's* Ulysses (1980), Elliott B. Gose, Jr., suggests that Bruno and Freud are integral polarities in the thought and art of this novel, Freud, like Bergson, representing psychological time and Bruno idealistic or spiritual.[41]

Even more recent is Jackson I. Cope's *Joyce's Cities: Archaeologies of the Soul* (1981), which links archaeological discovery to artistic gestation, a view which, Cope tells us, Joyce learned from D'Annunzio.[42] Thus, all history may be seen in circular form, and the stream of life as possessing accordingly no sequential pattern but becoming rather "a simultaneous polyexpression of the world." Like Gose, Cope shows that *Ulysses* is both mythic and mystic and treats

these focuses in conjunction with one another rather than as opposing factors. One is reminded here of descriptions of Freud's working
quarters in Vienna, filled with innumerable objects from antiquity.
Twenty statuettes were arranged on Freud's desk, neither by subject, period nor culture—ancient Greek or Roman next to Egyptian
or Chinese. This archaeological jumble represented, of course, the
kind of polyexpression described by Cope, events in time crowded in
a disorganized heap into the unconscious mind of race or individual.

Nor can one omit mentioning the special issue of the *James Joyce
Quarterly* in 1979 devoted to structuralist matters and reader response.[43] Here Jean Ricardou establishes two distinct levels, "the
time of the narration" and "the time of the fiction," as his basis for
discussion. He concludes that writing and architecture are contradictory magnitudes placed face to face, and fiction is the mediator in
this conflict.[44] Other important essays in this same issue deal with
similar problems of textuality. Thomas Staley, writing in the introduction, remarks that they open up the question of narrative "in
ways which reflect many recent developments," recognizing the influence that theories emanating from France and Eastern Europe
have exerted on the "Anglo-American critical consciousness." But
such matters as "deep structure," "deconstruction," and "reader response," as Staley notes, "have diminished as battle cries and have
become terms for serious discussion on the nature of the text and its
relationship to the author, reader, and the vast body of literature in
which it resides."[45] More seminal work remains to be done in this
field and in these areas. In addition, a more detailed examination of
mystical influences on Joyce's interpretation of time needs to be
carried out. Bruno of Nola and Nicholas of Cusa merit further study,
but Far Eastern sources have been largely neglected in this respect
and deserve attention. Furthermore, Joyce's interest in esotericism
is a wide-open field whose exploration should give us insight into
the archaeological past that Jackson Cope has begun to uncover in
his recent volume, where he attributes elaborations of the *Ulysses*
structures to cabbalistic texts and to key images in the *Zohar*. However, studies on the Viconian ages and the stream of consciousness in

the Joycean canon are by and large definitive, and have earned a rest, at least until the "commodius vicus of recirculation" returns critics to "Howth Castle and Environs" (*FW* 3.2—3), "where oranges have been laid to rust upon the green since devlinsfirst loved livvy" (*FW* 3.23—24).

Notes

1. (New York: Scribner's, 1950).

2. Tindall, p. 65. Ellsworth G. Mason's unpublished Yale dissertation, "Joyce's *Ulysses* and the Vico Cycle," preceded Tindall's study by two years.

3. Tindall, p. 84.

4. Tindall, p. 93.

5. "Mythic Mazes in *Finnegans Wake*," *Saturday Review of Literature*, 4 March 1950, p. 19.

6. "A Shout in the Street," *New Directions*, No. 13 (1951), pp. 327—45.

7. "Homer: Vico: Joyce," *Kansas Magazine* (1956), 83—88.

8. "Space-Time Polarity in *Finnegans Wake*," *Modern Philology*, 54 (1957), 20—33.

9. Kumar, p. 230.

10. Humphrey, *Stream of Consciousness in the Modern Novel* (Berkeley: Univ. of California Pr., 1954); Meyerhoff, *Time in Literature* (Berkeley: Univ. of California Pr., 1955); Friedman, *Stream of Consciousness: A Study in Literary Method* (New Haven: Yale Univ. Pr., 1955).

11. Meyerhoff, pp. 39—40.

12. Meyerhoff, p. 81.

13. *Bergson and the Stream of Consciousness Novel* (New York: New York Univ. Pr., 1963), p. 107.

14. *A New Approach to Joyce: A Portrait of the Artist as a Guidebook* (Berkeley: Univ. of California Pr., 1962).

15. Ryf, p. 98.

16. Ryf, p. 105.

17. Church, *Time and Reality* (Chapel Hill: Univ. of North Carolina Pr., 1963).

18. "A Viconian Sentence in *Ulysses*," *Orbis Litterarum*, 19 (1964), 201—4.

19. Hodgart, p. 203.

20. "Vico and Joyce," in *Giambattista Vico: An International Symposium*, ed. Giorgio Tagliacozzo and Hayden V. White (Baltimore: Johns Hopkins Univ. Pr., 1969), pp. 245—55.

21. Litz, p. 247.

22. Litz, p. 248.

23. Litz, p. 251.

24. "*Dubliners* and Vico," *James Joyce Quarterly*, 8 (1968), 150–56.

25. Ed. Thomas F. Staley and Bernard Benstock (Pittsburgh: Univ. of Pittsburgh Pr., 1976), pp. 77–89.

26. Ed. J. T. Fraser, N. Lawrence, D. Park (New York: Springer-Verlag, 1978), III, 500–11.

27. In *James Joyce Today*, ed. Thomas F. Staley (Bloomington: Indiana Univ. Pr., 1966), pp. 135–65; Hart's earlier work, of course, is *Structure and Motif in Finnegans Wake* (Evanston, Ill.: Northwestern Univ. Pr., 1962).

28. Hart, "*Finnegans Wake* in Perspective," pp. 164, 165.

29. (Baltimore: Johns Hopkins Univ. Pr., 1976).

30. "The Function of Mythic Repetition in *Finnegans Wake*," *James Joyce Quarterly*, 11 (1974), 347, 353.

31. "Vico's Institution of Burial in *Ulysses*," *Ball State University Forum*, 14 (1973), 59–68.

32. White, pp. 59–60.

33. "Joyce and Vico: The Middle Way," *New York Review of Books*, 18 October 1973, pp. 8–21.

34. Hampshire, pp. 21, 16, 14.

35. "Joyce's Use of Time in *Dubliners*," *Ball State University Forum*, 14 (1973), 51.

36. "The Stream of Consciousness Technique and the Structure of Joyce's *Portrait*," *James Joyce Quarterly*, 9 (1971), 63–84.

37. (Pittsburgh: Univ. of Pittsburgh Pr., 1973).

38. Steinberg, pp. 8–10.

39. *Ulysses* (London: George Allen and Unwin, 1980).

40. *Montage in Joyce's* Ulysses (Madrid: José Porrúa Turanzas, 1980).

41. (Toronto: Univ. of Toronto Pr., 1981).

42. (Baltimore: Johns Hopkins Univ. Pr., 1981).

43. Structuralist/Reader Response Issue, *James Joyce Quarterly*, 16 (1978/79).

44. "Time of the Narration, Time of the Fiction," trans. Joseph Kestner, *James Joyce Quarterly*, 16 (1978/79), 7–15.

45. Staley, "Introduction," *James Joyce Quarterly*, 16 (1978/79), 5.

7

FRITZ SENN

Foreign Readings

His language, so familiar and so foreign. . . .

Most of those whose native language is not English and who still want to weather Joyce's works will have asked themselves resignedly whether they have a chance to cope at all. The obvious answer, in one essential sense, is No; a handicap, not to be overcome, will remain. But it is a "No, But. . . ." And it is the various buts which will be butted about here.

As a rule, foreign readers will deviate to that substitute for the original text which replaces each of its single items and turns the whole into quite a different arrangement of letters and sounds while pretending to retain somehow its soul or spirit. What happens in translation will therefore deserve some passing attention here. In a much larger sense, everything Joyce wrote has to do with translation, is transferential.

Joyce had to read Homer in English, but he learned Norwegian to study Ibsen, applied his poor German to read Gerhart Hauptmann, while his Italian gave him access to Giordano Bruno and Vico. Foreigners are underprivileged, but they have one advantage: they know that the language is strange and has to be looked at very closely. A few close looks will be spread out here in the following pages as examples of the sort of naive wonder which native speakers may well have lost. Anything watched from a distance, from outside, can be exotically fascinating. Joyce felt this fascination himself and made others feel it. He profited from it. He fared better, on the whole, with friends in Trieste, international refugees in Zurich, or a mixed clique in Paris than with his compatriots, say Dublin cronies or English publishers. The roll call of early perceptive foreign readers includes Italo Svevo, Stefan Zweig, Valery Larbaud, Louis Gillet, Ernst Robert Curtius, Carola Giedion-Welcker, Bernhard Fehr, Hermann Broch, *et al*(*ieni*) and is proportionally impressive, especially in an early stage, that is, before Americans reclaimed him for the English–speaking world.

The foreign observer is an old literary device, since the outsider notices what is taken for granted by the member of a community. Joyce has varied this theme in all his works. Leopold Bloom is by no means the only one within this tradition, nor the first one in the canon.

Joyce's earliest story, "The Sisters," features an unnamed boy who becomes something of a foreign reader within the first paragraph, as he remembers words which "sounded strangely in [his] ears" (*D* 9). Their strangeness is indeed prominent, their shape odd, their meaning unguessable: it does not emerge from the context. "*Paralysis*" (from Greek, a "loosening beside"), "*gnomon*" (also Greek, "someone who knows"), and "*simony*" have to be defined first.[1] It was Euclid who determined, somewhat arbitrarily, because of its shape—via *gnomon* as a term for a sundial and then a carpenter's rule—what a gnomon is.[2] This is not how words normally acquire their meanings. A pre-Euclidian Greek would have been as puzzled by its geometrical sense as any 19th century schoolboy. And true to its nature, the Catechism lays down what "simony" is, an offense for which one Simon once set a bad precedent.

Part of the fascination of these three uncanny verbal beings is their primary opaqueness. (Have in mind also that one would not be sure, offhand, how to pronounce any of these words; Father Flynn, similarly, had to instruct the boy in proper Latin pronunciation.) They appeal to one's curiosity, a curiosity which has yielded rich critical rewards. In fact, a reader/critic has a way of becoming a *gnomon* right away: "an examiner, a judge, an interpreter."[3] Joyce opens with an appropriate conjunction: geometrically, "gnomon" is defined by something missing. The knowledge of an examining reader is indeed defective, incomplete. More mysteries remain unsolved in the story than there are reliable facts.

Once we inspect foreign territory we tend to find, or construe, more than we originally suspected. In Joyce's prose, this is a characteristic experience. Simony takes us straight to the account in the *Acts of the Apostles* and to Simon, who was one among about a dozen biblical persons of that name, a very common one. The name incidentally is based on a Hebrew verb for "hear": Sim(e)on is one who hears or obeys. Should we therefore deduce that hearing is particularly important? Maybe not, but the story is full of strange sounds, much hearsay and rumor, and contains audible silences. Our Simon, distinguished as "Magus," had his name perpetuated because of his misdeed and became famous, perversely, by doing wrong. The story of Father Flynn, too, is worth telling because something went wrong in his life. Immediately before Simon Magus is introduced into the biblical report, we read that "unclean spirits . . . came out of many that were possessed . . . and many taken with palsies and that were lame, were healed . . ." (Acts 8 : 7 − 8). Now "unclean spirits"—*pneumata akatharta* in the original[4]—can be interlaced with another foreign term in the story, Old Cotter's "talking of faints and worms" (*D* 10). "Faints" in distillery terminology are "impure spirits." Such alignment may amount to nothing more than a circuitous reconfirmation of some spiritual debasement in Father Flynn's career, but such subterranean short-circuiting is typical of Joyce's later work. The English "palsies" in the passage quoted derives from *paralysis*; the original used a participle *paralelymenoi*, whereas the Vulgate retains *paralytici*. So the words brought together in the protagonist's mind by chance association are contextually related in a source—as though a minor New Testament cluster were somehow buried within the story's opening signals, concealed by conspicuous foreignness.

Naturally this whole reading is foreign in yet another, radical sense: a *foranus* was someone who was *foras*, "outside of the doors," an outsider who is likely to use all his wits. Like a boy, for example, who, as he cannot know what goes on inside, "studied the lighted square of window" (*D* 9), as the second sentence in the story puts it.

Much of Joyce's meaning is, and has been from the start, somewhat outside the doors or at least a trifle removed. A near synonym of "foreign(er)" is based on the same spatial metaphor: *Stranger*, French *étranger*, derives from Latin *"extraneus,"* external, from *"extra,"* outside, without. Joyce's works are very much the saga of those without, of outsiders. It has become customary to refer to a certain kind of outsider by a different term stressed by Joyce: exile. The image is similar: an exile sits (or leaps) outside.

In view of what Joyce was to do later with names, we may think it remarkable that Simon, right after his ill-conceived offer of money for spiritual power, was rebuked by Peter himself (Acts 8:20–21), Peter on whose own name "the whole complex and mysterious institutions of the Church" were to be founded, as Joyce often rubbed in.[5] What makes this intriguing is that the misguided sorcerer and new convert was told off by a namesake, for Peter himself was also called Simon (Mat. 4:18). Father Flynn in the story seems to have hovered between the polar opposites of Simon Peter, first pope, and Simon Magus, an early debaser. The name Simon, at any rate, was to be carried over into the next two of Joyce's novels.

Of course no reader need ever engage in such alien philologistics. Yet the text invites some such loosening (*lysis*) aside (*para*) of the more outstanding elements which, as often as not, have a foreign appearance. Foreign words or phrases ask for a special effort, for some assimilation.

In *A Portrait* Stephen Dedalus has to face strange phenomena and strange languages. It is a discovery in itself that there *are* other languages. *"Dieu* was the French for God and that was God's name too; and when anyone prayed to God and said *Dieu* then God knew at once that it was a French person that was praying . . ." (*P* 16). One may be punished for not knowing the plural of the Latin noun *mare*.[6] But one's own language can be just as mysterious. "Suck," an ugly sound, like dirty water going out of a washbasin, is "a queer word," especially when applied to a "fellow" called Simon Moonan (*P* 11).

Like hardly any previous novel, *A Portrait* weaves the difficult empirical processes of learning the names of simple things and the curious ways in which grownups use words. We may overlook such an everyday quality as "nice," which clearly means something good or pleasant. Mother has "a nicer smell" than father; it is "nice and warm" to see a light. But there is more. "Rump" is "not a nice expression" (*P* 9), an unpleasant one, perhaps, but there intrudes an uneasy feeling of morality, of a superior world's rulings which may appear capricious; this world rules that reality will divide into things and into words for them, some of which are approved and some of which are not. It is not always an obvious distinction. When a pious relative, Mrs. Riordan, in angry conflict calls a snappy reply to a priest "A nice answer," surely she cannot approve? And her savage reduplication, "Very nice! Ha! Very nice!" (*P* 37), undoubtedly means that she is outraged about Mr. Casey's spitting tobacco juice into the eyes of a devout Irish woman. Young Stephen, a shocked and terrified listener, realizes that words can mean their own opposite, miraculously. Not all cultures, we know, allow for this kind of rhetoric. We could discover more linguistic runs in the novel hinging on other adjectives; an instructive one is "right" in the first chapter. Only trial and error teach us to handle or understand such labels. It is part of our survival strategies to master the use of words.

Even such ordinary learning processes will become something else when they are translated into languages where it is not possible to stick to the same adjective consistently, and so outside impressions gain more weight than society's verbal tags for them. A simple listing of the eight first occurrences of "nice" on only four opening pages will bear this out. Compare

a nicens little boy . . . a nicer smell . . . nice expression . . . Nice mother . . . a nice mother . . . not so nice . . . nice and warm . . . nice sentences,[7]

with Ludmilla Savitzky's translation of 1924:

un mignon petit garçon . . . plus agréable . . . une expression convenable . . . Gentille mère . . . gentille . . . moins gentille . . . bon et chaud . . . de jolies phrases;[8]

and with Dámaso Alonso's Spanish version (1926):

un niñín may guapín . . . olía mejor . . . expresión no estaba muy bien
. . . Madre querida . . . (next two not rendered) . . . agradable y reconfor-
tante . . . frases tan bonitas;[9]

and with Cesare Pavese's Italian translation of 1933:

un ragazzino carino . . . un odore più buono . . . una bella espressione
. . . Mammina bella . . . una mamma cara . . . non più cosí cara . . . dava
calore . . . belle frasi.[10]

Later readers are more aware of verbal structurings, as shown by
comparing an early German translation (Georg Goyert, 1926):

netten, kleinen Jungen . . . roch besser . . . hässliche Worte . . .
Hübsche Mutter . . . hübsche Mutter . . . nicht mehr so schön . . . es tat
so wohl . . . schöne Sätze[11]

against a recent one (Klaus Reichert, 1972), where consistency is
given priority:

eine sönen tleinen Tnaben . . . roch schöner . . . kein schöner Ausdruck
. . . Die schöne Mutter . . . eine schöne Mutter . . . nicht so schön . . .
schön und warm . . . so schöne Sätze.[12]

Needless to say, retention of the same adjective/adverb is not a crite-
rion of quality. Even where the repetition is recognized as meaning-
ful (a recognition slow in coming), its exact reproduction, where
possible, would still have to be evaluated against optimal rendering
within each variant phrase. The translation will change in any case.

That we learn to master words is brought out in what is probably
the most condensed summation of a learning process in all fiction,
the opening section of A Portrait. An abridgement of early impacts,
it moves rapidly from words for simple things, easy to verify in the
outside world—like "Moocow" (an animal identified by its sound
"moo" happens to be named "cow"—a descriptive ad hoc composite
well adapted to a child's mind), "road," or "lemon platt"—to something as unreal and recondite as "Apologise" (P 7–8). The syntax
has moved along with it, just as fast, and with it the thinking ability from impressions to generalizations. "Apologise" is quite an
achievement, not easy to grasp by any standards: it is unEnglish in
sound and appearance, of four syllables and of obscure meaning, but

very powerful. It stands in fact for the alternative for some traumatic punishment that could *happen* to him because of an unintended offense. It is possible to ward off some awesome consequence by saying appropriate *words*. As it happens, all of this is even contained *in* this word, though Stephen does (and the reader need) not know this. To apologize is a procedure of doing away (*apo-*) some effect by words/ speech (*logos*). Its effective and etymological potency alone would qualify the word for Stephen to linger over it and the author to put it at the end of his first movement.

That *apologia* (a speech made in one's defense, as the ancients used it) also figures in the title of an influential self-justification by a famous Jesuit convert and founder of Dublin University may add resonances later on when John Henry Cardinal Newman is named as one of the inchoative artist's self-appointed models. *A Portrait* has been taken to be Joyce's fictionalized *Apologia pro Vita Sua* (as a young man), a partial truth. Perhaps it is more an "apologuise," in the more precise version of *Finnegans Wake* (414.16), a work which always tries to excuse itself for its own deviate existence and which, to go back to origins, manages to undo the import of its words by disturbing semantemes: *apo-logia* in this meaning too.

In a conversation much later in the novel a highly articulate Stephen Dedalus says of a Jesuit theologian, Suarez, that he "apologised" for Jesus, who "seems to have treated his mother with scant courtesy" (*P* 242). Here too the term goes beyond a vague sense of making excuses; it resurrects accurately an explanation of the apparent rudeness of Jesus Christ's remark to his mother: "Woman, what have I to do with thee?" (John 2:4). In the original, so the defense by Suarez and other commentators goes, this remark was polite and respectful, but when an Aramaic idiom has to be given in Greek or English, something may happen to its tone and its understanding. No translation is free of such alterations, and *A Portrait* indirectly acknowledges that fact. What the *Wake* calls Shem's "root language" (424.17) is at work early on, in the foreignness of a loan word like "apologise" with its unrestful implications.

What a foreign reader, teased and frustrated, tends to notice

much more is that words are words, the only prime reality in literature. This makes non-natives akin to Stephen, a wary reader of all
sorts of signs and signatures. It is brought home to him in a well-
remembered scene that the language of the Irish is not theirs, is the
Englishman's ". . . before it is mine." Stephen feels "unrest of
spirit," the causes of which are partly political and historical. The
natives were forced to adopt the language of the conqueror, so much
so that in the end their own had to be revived artificially. Of course
they also changed the language which was imposed upon them; they
unwittingly kept a substratum of Gaelic patterns and evolved many
idiosyncratic uses, so that English as We Speak It in Ireland (as a
namesake, P. W. Joyce, called it) remains noticeably distinct: "His
language, so familiar and so foreign, will always be for me an
acquired speech" (*P* 189). His soul frets "in the shadow of his
language."

English was always an acquired speech for Joyce, and a shadow of
this is over all of his works. Any foreign reader will sympathize. But
the coerced have sneaky ways. Stephen Dedalus, Shem, or Joyce (a
personal union is allowed this time) went to revert all this, perhaps
an Irishman's revenge. *His* English, that of the works to follow, will
appear more and more odd to the English masters; there will be more
and more foreign matter, unfamiliar liberties, outlandish features,
unknown arts. All the major works, incidentally, were written
while Joyce himself was a foreigner in "Trieste-Zürich-Paris," a condition which the course of the twentieth century turns more and
more into a norm rather than an exception.

Ulysses, when it made its much-heralded appearance in Paris,
1922, was certainly considered chaotic and exotic and was accepted,
if anything, more readily on the Continent than in Ireland or Great
Britain. That Ireland had made "a sensational re-entrance into high
European literature," as Valery Larbaud announced, must have
sounded much more convincing to international groups in Paris or
Berlin than to literati in Dublin like Shane Leslie, who replied with
an outburst of invective at the book itself as well as at its foreign
admirers. He emphasised "devilish drench . . . muckwritten tide

. . . or vomit," but did find consolation in the fact, taken for granted, that the general reader was "in no danger of understanding" the book and might escape corruption.[13] There was clearly a linguistic basis for this reaction too. A novel written in English and dealing with Irish matters was, by and large, pronounced less accessible by those for whom its language was not an acquired one. It was thought to be European, and the dispute over this in itself proves a blurring of national borders.

There is no reader of *Ulysses* for whom some passages are not, literally, foreign and for whom many have not remained unfamiliar for a long time. *Ulysses* is in need of glosses and many of them mere translations of alien phrases, and those published have not always been outstandingly reliable. Readers and characters often go wrong, often without noticing. *Ulysses* creates numerous situations that are akin to those of its readers. Examples could be picked almost at random.

Bloom holds forth on the beauties of the Italian language, which he does not understand, and has to be told that the speakers he overheard were "haggling over money." He reacts in two ways well known to foreigners. The first is disappointment, a sigh of resignation "at the inward reflection of there being more languages to start with than were absolutely necessary." He also recognizes the strange fascination, "the southern glamour that surrounds" Italian. This very quickly leads to Stephen's generalization that sounds, like names, are "impostures" (*U* 621–22).

Leopold Bloom's own plucky shot at the glamorous foreign tongue, *Belladonna voglio*," does not parse too well but reveals separate items which the reader has been conditioned to spell out in the course of the novel. "Voglio" is a verb which makes it possible for Bloom to stave off nightshades, painful emotions, behind a concern for correct pronunciation. Bloom's Italian radiates psychologically: we translate the Italian into fears and hopes. A related worry interferes with an attempt to digest an opera passage, also in Italian: "*Don Giovanni, a cenar teco/M'invitasti*" (*U* 179). One word proves intractable: "What does that *teco* mean? Tonight perhaps." This is doing reasonably well; it is how we ourselves often read, unaided, out of context: "tonight" often goes with "come to supper." But from our vantage point, we know what looms in his mind within "tonight's" expected events. We may also find that *teco* (with you) is a way of implying the old wisdom (which has been reapplied by psychoanalysis as well) that *de te fabula narratur*. Our thoughts are determined by our problems.

As a fumbling linguist, Bloom is cautious and tentative. We see him struggle with some Latin. Notice that he gives two variants of "*Corpus*," one semantic, one derivative: "Body. Corpse" (*U* 80). His rendering of "*In paradisum*," though not the most taxing endeavour, is circumspect: "Said he was going to paradise or is in paradise" (*U* 104); the characteristic "or," allowing for possibilities, is in itself superior to some impressive scholarly glosses of Latin phrases in print.[14] Bloom fends with foreign elements as best he can. A priest's word at the funeral service he registers as "*Domine-namine*" (*U* 103). This indicates insufficient attention; Bloom is looking rather than listening. If the mental echo were a "correct" form like "(*in*) *nomine Domini*," we would probably just read on, unruffled; the scramble of word order, vowels and inflections, however, may make us pause. Bloom's re-creation is neatly parallel. Perhaps the correct vocative, "*Domine*," heard elsewhere, is included. No doubt the English "name," a cognate, interferes with "*nomine*." Bloom has just been thinking: "Father Coffey. I knew his name was like coffin," and perhaps the word more or less coincided with the Latin equivalent, so that "*namine*" might not be faulty, but a carryover. The point is not that the extrication just given is valid, but that we are provoked into giving some account of the confusion. A few hours later, when Bloom overhears "*in nomine Dei*" as part of "The Croppy Boy," the words become, in his mind, "*in nomine Domini*" (*U* 284).[15] Latin, Bloom muses, "holds them like birdlime," and we observe that his mind sticks to certain phrases too. He conjures up a memory from Glasnevin cemetery and an earlier visit to a church: "*corpusnomine*," a conflation of previous echoes. Botched foreign phrases have a way of holding us too, the readers, like birdlime, and Bloom's own composite insinuates that names/nouns have an almost physical being. Foreigners are often seduced by the body of words. "Pyrrhus, a pier" (*U* 24) we can take to be a corpusnominal association.

Molly Bloom is not alone in interpreting "polysyllables of foreign origin . . . phonetically or by false analogy" (*U* 686). Bloom misinterprets Fergus, mythological figure from a Yeats poem, as "Ferguson . . . Some girl. Best thing could happen him" (*U* 608–9). Readers are not immune to such imaginative leaps. Let us return to Bloom in the mortuary chapel as he watches the priest and tries to assimilate some of the Latin from the sermon in between. "*Dominenamine*. Bully about the muzzle he looks. Bosses the show" (*U* 103). One might be forgiven for imagining, one moment, some Latin ox or cow (*bos*) in "Bosses," for which there is no philological foundation; and one might wonder if there is an accidental bull in "Bully." A native reader, if asked, most probably would "know" instinctively whether there is or not. What *does* Bloom have in mind? The *Oxford English Dictionary* notices that "popular etymological consciousness" tends to connect the two words.

Readers can shrug their shoulders and go on, but not so translators; they have to put something down and therefore must make decisions. Of the two authorized translations, the German one keeps close to the animal while still getting the impression of someone powerful and overbearing: "Ums Maul sieht er bullig aus." The French version is based on quite different considerations: "Un fort en gueule, ça se voit." Nothing bullish there; the characterization stresses grossness and even verbosity. A later Italian translation suggests a blustering fellow: "Ha un muso di prepotente." This triple divergence proves nothing more than potential ambivalence; associations detected in the sentence are magnified.

The "correct" solution, one might argue, is the one provided in a reference work, Eric Partridge's *Dictionary of Slang and Unconventional English*, which says: "*bully about the muzzle. 'Too thick and large in the mouth'* . . . *dog-fanciers'* . . ."[16] So the phrase predates Bloom and had become stereotyped. There is a certain probability that originally the dog-fanciers who coined the saying were struck by a bull-like appearance. Tossing a phrase about, we may notice here, usually leads not to more clarity but to more complexity. The results of the above probe are merely that a word may well participate in two semantic activities. "Bully" would go well with Father Coffey as a "muscular christian"; "bull-y" contributes to a cluster of animal imagery for the priest (who doubles as Cerberus in Hades): "his toad's belly . . . said the rook . . . a fluent croak . . . Bully . . . (Bosses?) . . . sheep . . . poisoned pup" (*U* 103). It occurs midway between a dog transformed by Stephen's mind in Proteus and the animal metamorphoses of Circe.

All the speculations just given as mere illustrations may appear a trifle less gratuitous when we find a passage much later which looks like—but cannot realistically be—a reshuffling of Bloom's thoughts spiced by dog Latin. In Oxen of the Sun, where avatars tend to be bovine, a long tale about Pope Hadrian's generosity to England is spun out, and in it an initial papal bull is turned into a browsing animal with features of a bullying John Bull. In the course of this homonymous festival we come across "the famous champion bull of the Romans, *Bos Bovum*, which is good bog Latin for boss of the show" (*U* 401). This appears as though the bodies of words had changed from Dublin street wear to Roman togas or priestly vestments—transformations that do occur in both Oxen and Circe. Or words here change their nationality (as Bloom's father did). In *Finnegans Wake* something like "bull, a bosbully" (*FW* 490.35) would cause little surprise and only show once more that words have turned this condition into a way of life.

Since *Ulysses* transversally encloses a cheeky permutation of "Bully: bull: boss: *bos*," we may digress for a while to observe what happens when such process itself has to be translated. Since the two passages are so distant and the connection tenuous, chances are that translators did not recognize it and (let us bear in mind) perhaps need not acknowledge it in their assessment of priorities. To give a better idea of what dexterity would ideally be called for to recreate a text's low-key correspondences, two more instances of "bully" are listed, one in the Library episode, where Stephen gives examples of

"Women he won to him . . . bully tapsters' wives" (*U* 193). In this phrase "bully" is a character trait, and the translations consulted all agree that it qualifies "tapsters" and not their wives. In themselves versions like "des épouses de cabaretiers brutaux," "spose di rozzi tavernieri," or "prahlender Zapfkellner Weiber," would not be worth much comment. Only the second German rendering (1976) retains the adjective which was used by Bloom in the morning, "bulliger Zapfkellner Weiber," and it alone would catch a potential Pasiphaean echo, if there should be one (to reinforce Stephen's "queens with prize bulls"—*U* 207). What all foreign renderings miss, however, is what in this chapter may not be negligible—that in older, and Shakespearean, parlance, "bully" was also a term of endearment.

A treacherous "bully" appears in Oxen of the Sun, as if to confuse the issues even more. "But they can go hang . . . for me with their bully beef" (*U* 398). The beef in question is "Kerry cows," so we have here a tricky misuse of the phrase "bully beef," in which "bully" derives from French *bouilli*, but is tied to "beef" (related to Latin *bos*). It is interesting to see which translations opt for a form of potted meat, and which ones have diminutive cattle romping about, alive and kicking: "avec leur barbaque de cambuse"; "mit ihrem verseuchten Büchsenfleisch";[17] "e i loro torelli baldanzosi," etc.

The dispersed bits of text and how they appear in several languages are tabulated here (pp. 96–97) for convenient comparison. The focus is on one of Bloom's thoughts and how it seems to radiate. The sample translations are arranged vertically in chronological order.

Given the tremendous odds, the translations emerge with credit. We see more awareness of transverse links in later renderings, when the novel was better known and the importance of correspondences more recognized. But in any foreign tongue *Ulysses* becomes less interstructured. Much of the bovinity which shapes Joyce's ends does not travel too well.[18] What translation can deal with least is translation itself, like "boss—*bos*," where an identical choreography of equivalents is excluded by a different vocabulary. We may appreciate French "latin de latrine," which imitates "bog Latin" as derived from "bog(-house)," privy, by substituting *latrine* for a more current "*latin de cuisine.*" A felicity like the original phrase itself, which suitably brings dog Latin home to bogland (Ireland), can hardly be expected.

The do-it-yourself exercise attempted here is intended also to show native readers that, while they try out switchboard connections and are forced to reflect on what the text may try to say, they are in fact behaving like foreigners in search of sense and meaning. The perspectives given here, and the way the cards have been stacked against translators, are highly unfair and amount to a falsification. The bullockbefriending collocations may be valid by being part of the novel's intricate potential, but they are only a few among many. The above approach is as instructive and as misleading as any other. The translations should therefore be appreciated by quite different criteria, such as "accuracy" (by now, it is hoped, a somewhat shaky notion), tonal effect, or idiomatic punch.

Up to a point, *Ulysses* makes stridently clear (in the original or in translation) that we are all foreigners lost in a labyrinth. The main characters feel unacclimatized at best. Marion Bloom, with an obscure Spanish-Jewish mother named Lunita Laredo, is apt to pass judgment on Dublin in view of her childhood memories in colonial Gibraltar. Bloom's lost roots go back to Hungary and a Jewishness from which he is also excluded. Stephen Dedalus sees himself dispossessed. These topics need no further elaboration in 1982. In day-to-day transactions it is not so much the lack of foreign languages that causes misunderstanding, but our different perspectives or expectations, the various codes existing side by side. Dialogues are often at cross purposes (Stephen and Mr Deasy; Bloom and Bantam Lyons; much of the talking in Barney Kiernan's). This becomes most poignant when Leopold Bloom and Stephen Dedalus are finally brought together (which, in our novel–reading code, should become a climax) and some talk is attempted, largely by Bloom, but little communication occurs. Some of the conversation might almost be conducted in different languages.

Bloom in the morning carefully and resiliently translates a diffi-

their bully beef (*U* 398)	bully tapsters' wives (*U* 193)	Bully about the muzzle he looks. Bosses the show. (*U* 103)
leur barbaque de cambuse (386)	des épouses de cabaretiers brutaux (185)	Un fort en gueule, ça se voit. Le grand manitou de l'affaire. (98)
mit ihrem verseuchten Büchsenfleisch (449)	prahlender Zapfkellner Weiber (220)	Ums Maul sieht er bullig aus. Schwingt die Fuchtel. (120)
med sin oxestek (404)	frodiga vintapparkvinnor (201)	Köttig om nosen. Chef för teatern. (110)
e i loro torelli baldanzosi (539)	spose di rozzi tavernieri (262)	Ha un muso da prepotente. È il padrone del vapore. (145)
met hun vlees in blik (462)	de vrouwen van bullebakken van tappers (226)	Wat een bullebak met zo'n muil. De baas van het spul. (121)
mit ihrem Weckfleisch (559)	bulliger Zapfkellner Weiber (271)	Bullig ums Maul sieht er aus. Schmeisst die ganze Chose. (146)
con sus novillos y todo (II, 41)	mujeres de taberneros chulos (I, 325)	Tiene cara de chulo con esa jeta. Domina la función. (I, 206)

the famous champion bull of the
Romans, *Bos Bovum*, which is
good bog Latin for boss of the
show. (*U* 401)

Ulysses
(New York: Random House,
1961)

du fameux taureau champion des
Romains, *Bos Bovum*, qui signifie
en bon latin de latrine le patron
de la boîte. (395)

Ulysse (1929)
tr. Auguste Morel, assisté de
Stuart Gilbert, entièrement revue
par Valery Larbaud et par l'auteur
(Paris: Gallimard, 1948)

des berühmten Preisbullen der
Römer war, des *Bos Bovum*, was in
gutem Latrinenlatein Besitzer der
Bude bedeutet.[19] (452)

Ulysses (1927/1930)
tr. Georg Goyert vom Verfasser
geprüfte Uebersetzung
(Zurich: Rhein Verlag, 1956)

av den berömda mästertjuren i
Rom, *Bos Bovum*, vilket är gott
kökslatin för överstebov. (407)

Odysseus (1964)
tr. Th. Warburton
(Stockholm: Albert Bonniers
Förlag, 1964)

del famoso toro campione dei ro-
mani, *Bos Bovum*, che significa in
buon *latinorum*, padrone del va-
pore. (543)

Ulisse (1960)
tr. Giulio di Angelis; consulenti:
Glauco Cambon, Carlo Izzo,
Giorgio Melchiori
(Milan: Arnoldo Mondadori, 1960)

die beroemde stier der Romeinen,
Bos Bovum, wat in goed rioollatijn
betekent baas van het spul. (464)

Ulysses (1969)
tr. John Vandenbergh
(Amsterdam: De Bezige Bij, 1969)

des berühmten Preisbullen der
Römer, *Bos Bovum*, . . . was gutes
Küchenlatein ist und heisst ver-
dolmetscht Der Boss vons Janze.
(562)

Ulysses (1976)
tr. Hans Wollschläger
(Frankfurt: Suhrkamp, 1976)

del famoso toro campeón de los
romanos, *Bos Bovum*, lo que en
buen latín macarronico quiere de-
cir el amo del cotarro. (II, 44)

Ulises (1976)
tr. J. M. Valverde
(Barcelona: Editorial Lumen,
1976)

cult word of Greek origin to his wife, a word he first has to extract from a Mollyesque assimilation, "Met him. . . ." He first chooses a key too high and intellectual, "transmigration," which is scoffed at ("O rocks! . . . tell us in plain words"). Then he solicitously prepares for another hard word, "reincarnation," by homely phrasing ("some people believe . . . that we go on living in another body after death. . . .") while thinking of a suitable graphic illustration (*U* 64–65). In the Eumaeus episode with roles reversed, this considerate man, usually so much aware of the grasp of his audience, is exposed to statements jerkily expressed by Mr. Dedalus, poet and professor, who all along has shown supreme disregard for his listeners. So paternal Bloom misses the patristic jargon of "soul" as "a simple substance," and responds in terms of X-rays and "simple souls" (*U* 633–34). Let us try to imagine just what it might be that Bloom actually registers when he is treated to the following discourse:

the lutenist Dowland who lived in Fetter Lane near Gerard the herbalist, who *anno ludendo hausi, Doulandus*, an instrument he was contemplating purchasing from Mr Arnold Dolmetsch . . . and Farnaby and son with their *dux* and *comes* conceits and Byrd (William), who played the virginals . . . and one Tomkins who made toys or airs and John Bull. (*U* 661–62)

We have it on good authority that Bloom is understandably misdirected by "John Bull." As for the rest we can only guess. Bloom is "not perfectly certain" (*U* 662); he must be shut out, "out of doors," from most of this. The Latin is beyond him (might he hear something like "lewdhouse"?); "*dux*" is likely to sound like something in English which it is not; and what is a casual listener to make of fetter, bird, or toys? In one wrong sense, "conceits" is right. The names themselves must be cryptic. "Farnaby and son" sounds like a Dublin firm and not like historical composers. As Bloom is not an expert on ancient instruments, nor a reader of Joyce's *Letters* or Richard Ellmann's biography, he has no way of knowing who Arnold Dolmetsch is.[20] It is a tantalizing touch that, when so much non-communication is around, Joyce throws out the name of a real person whose name in German, if it were understood, would mean exactly what at this juncture is most needed between the two, an "interpreter."

When in the next chapter some interchange of speech and of ideas finally does occur between the two different temperaments, it is ironically removed from our reach by its presentation in a form of abstract, scientific, unfelt English which is pointedly written, never spoken. We will mentally change this language into the sort of idiom which it is meant to replace. Runs like "disintegration of obsession" (*U* 695) will normally be rendered into something else within the same language, something very painful and direct. One psychological justification for "Ithaca" is that it keeps emotions at a Latinate distance. The mode of "Ithaca" is one last variant of the many intralingual translations in *Ulysses*. The book exposes not only a wide range of languages, but also the regional, temporal, social, and hierarchical width of the English language. Joyce in particular adds historical diversification. In one episode which describes a librarian as "bald, eared and assiduous" (*U* 190), it is odd to come upon "singular uneared wombs" (*U* 202). We get an almost surrealist effect. This is continued two chapters later with similar anatomic confusion: "womb of woman eyeball" (*U* 286). But, naturally, "uneared" does does not denote an absence of the organs of hearing but is an obsolete recall, through a Shakespearean echo, of an Indo-European verb for ploughing (cognate with Latin *arare*). The semantic shock will spur us on to translate it into our own time.[21]

Ulysses is probably the first consistently intertransferential fictional work. Oxen of the Sun manifests this aspect best and most irritatingly, in a historical series of literary devices and linguistic growth. Not only have morphology and syntax changed over the centuries, but also customs and mores, attitudes, conventions, epical techniques and narrative emphases—the most radical, continuous intratranslation. No wonder this chapter is still the least assimilated one, and one impossible to translate "adequately." In some critical dismissals of its idiosyncrasies we may still detect a streak of that mentality which Joyce, after all, has thematized, that whatever is foreign is unnecessary or arbitrary, if not downright inferior.

The chapter modes of *Ulysses* are, in the view presented here, so many different translations, renderings in keys that could be labelled breezy, gastronomical, literary, locative, orchestral, polyphemous, daydreamy, etc., and the separate labels matter less than the idea of a conjugation of all of language's potential and all stylistic ranges. We do not need "*Introibo ad altara Dei*" as an initial pointer, nor a blatant hybrid like "Deshil Holles Eamus" as a midway reminder, nor a farewell display of "Ronda . . . posadas" (*U* 782), to learn, the hard way, what Bloom has always known, that we are in certain constellations aliens and fumbling outsiders. The foreign reader simply notices this plight a trifle more tangibly.

As always, proportions change when we come to *Finnegans Wake*. There non-English readers are truly lost, especially since they rely on their eyes and their ability to spell out graphic shapes more than on their ears for hidden sounds in hidden words. The lack of childhood echoes, sayings, songs, nursery rhymes, etc., is a severe drawback. Foreigners may take some slight comfort in the fact, freely confessed, that native readers remain in the dark as well when they have to sort out so much that is unfamiliar and alien, and above all when they have to extract their own language from the circumambient verbiage. In a conglomerate like "perensempry sex of fun to help a dazzle off the othour" (*FW* 364.24), we may detect Latin words, sex, perhaps saxophone, long before the author's dazzle also reveals a homely phrase, "six of one and half a dozen of the other." At least it is indicated by ancillary works that such back-renderings are indeed necessary.[22]

Paradoxically, the *Wake* is the most forbiddingly xenophobic of all prose works, and yet at the same time it extends a catholic welcome to all foreigners by meeting them on their own territory, and very specifically. It often says so, in "wordloosed . . . in cellelleneteutoslavzendlatinsoundscript" (*FW* 219.16) addressing the Indo-European family; in other parts it speaks Japanese or Maori. It offers foreign readers snippets which perhaps only they can understand. A Swahili speaker can count ALP's children in "meanacuminamoyas" (*FW* 201.30), which somehow adds up to 111, and there is confirmation in Hebrew numerology appended: "Olaph lamm et, all that pack." An Irish reader would be struck by an ironic interjection, "-moya," which throws doubt on whatever was said before; that too is a Wakean linguistic caution. A Swiss, coming upon "mean fawthery eastend appullcelery, old laddy he high hole" (FW 586.27), may wonder what is being told about apples and celery in the eastend, but may recognize at some moment that the whole also transliterates a familiar dialect song, "Min Fatter ist en Appezäller," which simply says that "my father is from (the canton of) Appenzell." To detect something familiar in an exotic guise is a basic pleasure and an incentive. A little bit of rummaging may turn up the appropriateness of the name leading back to Latin "abbatis cella," the cell of the abbot (and abbas of course means father). The historical abbot in question was Irish, St. Gall, who was sent east to convert the heathen. Actually there is not just one canton called Appenzell, but two: the father's cell split up during some wars over religion, and a Wakean family configuration is here echoed in Swiss history and geography. Both Appenzells, looking almost fetally entwined on the map, are moreover wholly surrounded by the canton of St. Gall, like "wrestless in the womb" (FW 143.21)—all of which merely exemplifies Finnegans Wake's outstanding obligingness. A perfect provincial miniature has been integrated, which serves well to demonstrate to a purely Swiss audience some of the overall themes and dynamics. The next line will nationalize a standard figure of the Wake with more local colour: "Seekersenn" (FW 586.28) contains a name, Senn, which is very common (especially in the cantons mentioned), and also a noun which immediately evokes images of cows, cheese and butter (Senn is an alpine cowherd). This connects with a Swiss German incarnation of Shaun ("Haensli") and Shem ("Koebi") within the Burrus-Caseous entanglement (FW 163.5). The song which triggered off all these associations continues, as every Swiss would know, with the Appenzell father eating cheese. From all of this, meanwhile, the non-Swiss reader is largely excluded but will at least instantly click into tune when "old laddy he high hole" is revealed to be the yodelling refrain.

Of course the distinction between native and foreign has by now become very questionable and idle. Dublin is a good city, and Ireland a much-afflicted country, to bear this out. *Finnegans Wake* unravels and re-entangles colonial sedimentation through language. When native and invader crosstalk in French, donsk, scowegian, or anglease, and excheck a few strong verbs (*FW* 16.4–5), discrimination between settler and intruder, inhabitant and conqueror, seller or buyer, guest or enemy, is instantly rendered futile. A later re-enactment of a similar encounter, this time garbled by Muta and Juva, is similarly confused and polyglot (*FW* 609–10). Certainty becomes a matter of betting: "Tempt to wom Outsider!" (*FW* 610.18). Everyone—Firbolg, Milesian, Celt, Viking, Norman, Sassenach, or Jew—was once an outsider. "Paybads floriners moved in hugheknots" (*FW* 541.14) refers to a specific historical occasion, but it seems to generalize that foreigners, often refugees, have difficulties with their currencies and may be a nuisance or poor risks. It is again interesting that the Huguenots, a dispersed minority, got their name from a word meaning confederates (by oath, German *Eid-genoss*). Contrary to this implication, they were disbanded and persecuted, but then found new homes and, on the whole, adapted very well and were beneficial to their new communities. Words can have similar divaricating careers.

Finnegans Wake, with its hugheknots in polyglot, is solipsistic in speaking only to itself about itself. It is aristocratic in addressing small erudite elites, even though no single expertise gets any of them very far. *Finnegans Wake* is uniquely democratic and as global as UNESCO in accepting all of us and turning all of us into foreign readers, evoking that typical mixture of frustration and fascination. So that, though we still do not understand, we simply cannot let go.

Notes

1. One would have a rough idea of what all other words mean within that first paragraph simply from the company they keep. Even if one did not know the

meaning of "maleficent" (*D* 9), it could be approximately determined by its surroundings.

2. The phrasing "the Euclid" shows that this name has come to stand for a subject, or a book.

3. Meanings given by Liddell and Scott's *Greek-English Lexicon*. Further derivations used in this essay are of course (see *SH* 26, 30) from Walter W. Skeat, *An Etymological Dictionary of the English Language* (Oxford: Clarendon, 1879–82).

4. The Greek *pneuma* (for air, but also ghost, spirit) is later replaced by a disease in Eliza's uneducated phrase "one of them new-fangled carriages that makes no noise . . . them with the rheumatic wheels" (*D* 17). Verbal undercurrents of this kind were pointed out in my "He Was Too Scrupulous Always: Joyce's 'The Sisters,'" *James Joyce Quarterly*, 2 (1965), 189–95.

5. "[C]ertain institutions of the Church which I had always regarded as the simplest acts" (*D* 13). *Acts!* Later on Joyce was to use such words as clues or hidden pointers for his sources. Here it *could* be aptly coincidental.

6. Oddly enough, the plural form implied by absence, "*maria*," looks very much like the name of the Virgin in Latin.

7. *P* 7, 9, 10.

8. *Dedalus*, trans. Ludmilla Savitzky, 15th ed. (Paris: Gallimard, n.d.), pp. 17–20.

9. *El artista adolescente*, trans. Alfonso Donado [Dámaso Alonso], (Madrid: Editorial Biblioteca Nueva, 1963), pp. 27–30.

10. *Dedalus*, trans. Cesare Pavese (Milan: Adelphi Edizioni, 1976), pp. 3–6.

11. *Jugendbildnis*, trans. Georg Goyert (Zurich: Rhein Verlag, 1926), pp. 8–13.

12. *Ein Porträt des Künstlers als junger Mann*, trans. Klaus Reichert (Frankfurt: Suhrkamp, 1972), pp. 7–10. The form "sönen" represents childish mispronunciation.

13. "*Ulysses*," review by 'Domini Canis' (Shane Leslie), *Dublin Review*, Sept. 1922, rpt. in *James Joyce: The Critical Heritage*, ed. Robert H. Deming (London: Routledge & Kegan Paul, 1970), I, 200–3.

14. Don Gifford and Robert J. Seidman, *Notes for Joyce: An Annotation of James Joyce's* Ulysses (New York: Dutton, 1974), glosses "*Terribilia meditans*" (*U* 45) as "Terrible to mediate" (p. 42). It is not the misprint ("mediate" for "meditate") which is objectionable, but the syntactic ignorance which may be passed on.

15. Zack Bowen, who also notices that "*nomine Domini* . . . doesn't fit the tune," has a different view and attributes the "error" clearly to Joyce. See his *Musical Allusions in the Works of James Joyce* (Albany: State Univ. of New York Pr., 1974), p. 197.

16. In all fairness it has to be said that *A Ulysses Phrasebook*, by Helen H. Macaré (Portola Valley, Calif.: Woodside Prior, 1981), the sort of book that explains

the foreign parts of *Ulysses*, here offers a gloss which is acceptable and helpful: "beefy about the jaw" (p. 26). The *Phrasebook* is otherwise incredibly unreliable.

17. Translations, too, may bully each other. The German version of 1927 avoided the issue with a flat "mit all ihrem Fleisch" (Zurich: Rhein Verlag, II, 396). This was revised in 1930 and many subsequent printings to "können sie mit ihrem Ochsenlouis die Blattern dazu kriegen . . ." (1930, II, 28). Here "Louis" catches the meaning of a "protector of a prostitute" or "bully." A connection was probably established with "two shawls and a bully on guard" (*U* 314); the German for this was "mit zwei Fosen und ein Louis passt auf . . ." (p. 353)—a *possible* link. In a later "Sonderausgabe" in one volume ("Copyright 1956," according to its imprint), a different, third, version appears. The publishers accepted suggestions received in letters, with or (probably) without Georg Goyert's consent. In this case the French rendering, "leur barbaque de cambuse," most likely served as a guideline and correction, and in the process what is merely bad meat in French (and perhaps from another animal: one etymology of "barbaque" is a Rumanian word for "mutton"), is amplified to "infected"—"verseucht," a word which seems to have been induced by "Seuche," for "plague" (*U* 398).

18. Remember that it is a current theme in *A Portrait*, where Stephen gets the appellation "*Bous Stephanoumenos*" (*P* 168, *U* 210, 415). *Bous* is the Greek equivalent of Latin *bos*; Homer uses the plural "*boes*" for the oxen, or rather the kine, of Helios. Antiquity often brought gods and oxen, or bulls, together; the animals were sacrificed, there was taurine worship (as on Crete), and there is the proverbial contrast, "*Quod licet Jovi, non licet bovi.*" Consider also echoes like "Thou shalt not *muzzle* the mouth of an ox. . ." (Deut. 25:4), to which St. Paul adds a question: "Does God care for oxen?" (1 Cor. 9:9; the Vulgate uses a form of *bos*). We know that Helios, for one, did care about his cattle and that Odysseus was to suffer for it. Even Stephen's often quoted "*dio boia*, hangman god" which is "doubtless all in all in all of us. . ." (*U* 213) is rooted in this theme. The Italian *boia* for hangman goes back to a Greek adjective *boeios* (straps were once made from the hides of the animals). Homer mentions several such oxhides; one "*boeiê*" is described as "newly flayed" (*Odyssey* 22:363–64). We find exactly this in a Cyclopian translation, "garment of recently flayed oxhide" (*U* 296). It is the Citizen mock-epically exalted, and this famous bully (and compare our quote at *U* 401 with "Bullyfamous" in *FW* 229.15) has a hangman mentality. Joyce's early warning, "Don't play the giddy ox with me" (*U* 7) is justified.

19. The German version of 1927 was "*Bos Bovum*, welches ja für ihn in seiner Stellung ein vorzüglicher Name war" (II, 402); this is very vague and inexact. Its revised form again follows the French.

20. *Letters* I, 54; Richard Ellmann, *James Joyce*, pp. 159–61.

21. Once more *this* step does not translate. In exact Italian, "singoli venti non

arati" (p. 274), there is no disturbance nor any historical adjustment; the French version "touchant les pucelages récalcitrants" (p. 198), is a free paraphrase.

22. Roland McHugh, *Annotations to* Finnegans Wake (London: Routledge & Kegan Paul, 1980), p. 364; Dounia Bunis Christiani, *Scandinavian Elements of* Finnegans Wake (Evanston, Ill.: Northwestern Univ. Pr., 1965), p. 180, et passim.

8

SHELDON BRIVIC

Joycean Psychology

Aristotle defined the *psyche*, mind or soul, as the primary organization of knowledge in a living being (*De Anima*, 412). Without a mind to inform it, life disintegrates into unconnected phenomena, and so psychology implants a mind in its subject. To be unified, a mind must have continuous structural principles, but to be alive, or capable of change, it must combine different interacting forces. Joycean psychology aims to define the mental structures and activities involved in Joyce's work; to see these clearly, we must ask not only what kinds of psychic apparatus are found there, but where they are located in relation to the text.

The concept of mind as a dynamic interaction of forms and impulses is maintained today by the theories of psychoanalysis. This definition of mind is generally regarded as essential to understanding Joyce, and most psychological treatments of Joyce's work to date have been analytic. One exception, Erwin R. Steinberg's *The Stream of Consciousness and Beyond in* Ulysses, uses statistical analysis of verbal patterns to explain how Joyce represents cognition and association, differentiating the textures of thought of his protagonists. But when he wants to explain motivation in depth, Steinberg turns to an external psychoanalytic source. [1]

Significant human decisions involve agencies in the mind that influence each other qualitatively, impulses that change each other's natures. For this reason, the principles that make a psychological system mathematically precise tend to sunder it from real mental action. Of course, effort is being made to bridge the gap between mechanism and mentality. Douglas R. Hofstadter's relation of mathematics and creativity in *Gödel, Escher, Bach* has excited Joyceans and is likely to stimulate attempts to present Joycean mentality in cybernetic terms.[2] Such an approach rests on the fact that the mind in Joyce is an assemblage of words, but it may go astray in assuming that words are inanimate. At any rate, Joyce himself wondered if a being could be constituted out of a multiplicity of mathematical functions: "howmulty plurators made eachone in person?" (*FW* 215.25).

Another theory relevant to Joyceans is the bicameral psychology of Julian Jaynes, which is based on distinctions between brain lobes that suggest the differences between Shem and Shaun.[3] Finally, the cognitive psychology of Jean Piaget and others can explain stages of Stephen Dedalus's development and can clarify logical functions involved in Joyce's writing process.[4] I hope these non-analytic approaches can be brought in touch with the essential mental life of the novels.

So far, however, the psychology of Joyce has been largely psychoanalytic, and the vital interplay of such analysis seems to mesh with something central in Joyce. Lionel Trilling spoke for many early critics when he said in 1940 that of all modern novelists, Joyce "has perhaps most thoroughly and consciously exploited Freud's ideas."[5] Twenty years later the idea of Joyce as a follower of Freud seemed questionable, but it has now been confirmed. Perhaps the strongest indications against Freud appear in Richard Ellmann's *James Joyce*: though Ellmann psychoanalyzes Joyce in his eighteenth chapter, he presents a series of quotations from Joyce disparaging Freud throughout his biography, perhaps because he was struck by statements contradicting a common assumption.

From 1966 on, however, a stream of material has supported Trilling's opinion. The letters and personal writings in which Joyce recorded his sexual pathology in detail were followed by the line "Wit. read Freud" in the *Ulysses* notesheets.[6] Then came Arthur Power's *Conversations with James Joyce*, in which Joyce expresses his intention "to enlarge our vocabulary of the subconscious";[7] in *The Consciousness of Joyce*, Ellman reports that Joyce bought four books of

analysis from about 1910 to 1918.[8] As one of these was Freud's
Psychopathology of Everyday Life, we now know that Chester G. An-
derson was right when he said that Joyce systematically included in
Ulysses every kind of parapraxis listed by Freud.[9]

Though Joyce mocked the authority of psychoanalysis, he followed its ideas and saw their affinities with his own. The latest
source of his analytic thinking is the Joyce Archive. One important
passage occurs in one of the *Finnegans Wake* notebooks:

⟦ [the autobiographical Shem] identifies se with own penis
oral zone
observing a coitus
our littleman's
ego
totem [10]

If these lines are equated with each other, they mean the ego is a
phallus, a sensitive zone, a vision of terror and bliss, a god. This
would explain such elements as the tumescence and detumescence
techniques of the Nausicaa episode of *Ulysses*, by which the mind
works as a phallus. Like other notes, these are not a listing, but a
theorizing along lines of association posited by Freud.

If we grant that Joyce's definition of mind followed a Freudian
dynamic, the next step toward understanding the Joycean mind is to
ask where it is located. There are at least five levels of mind involved
in Joyce's enterprise: the mind of Joyce, those of the characters,
those of the readers, what Hugh Kenner calls the mind of the text,[11]
and the mind of the language. Each of these may be seen as plural if
we grant that language, text, and the individual mind may be divided. Shem is described as being "of twosome twiminds" (*FW*
188.14), adding up to four and rendering every opponent an "oc-
tagonist" (*FW* 174.17).

If each of the five mental levels of the work is related to itself and
to each of the others, fifteen combinations are possible, such as
reader to character, book to language, one character to another, and
Joyce to himself. There is every reason to believe that Joyce was
aware of all of these parts and relations and of how they operate in the

work. The psychology of each of these connections should be understood in terms of its position and its function in the Joyce world, rather than subjected to some overall scheme for the whole. Of course, some of these junctions represent better possibilities for study than others. For example, there is need for a study of the dynamic relation of the reader's mind to Joyce's text.[12] But the major need is for a theory of the relation of these positions to each other, and the abundant development they all receive in Joyce makes him an ideal subject on which to develop such a theory.

Having suggested one framework of possibilities, I would like to move toward the question of what kinds of minds we can locate in Joyce by a consideration of what has been done. In *Joyce in Nighttown*, the first psychoanalytic study of Joyce, Mark Shechner sees Joyce's personal writings and *Ulysses* as a series of gestures by which he related to himself. Shechner shows how Joyce made up for the loss of his mother and for his distance from Nora Barnacle by reconstituting his mother and Nora through his work as an internalized function. This function helped him gain control over his mind by allowing him to release perverse fantasies from his unconscious. Shechner, who uses ego psychology, sees Joyce's rational side progressively assimilating his irrational guilt and desire into a self-enclosed structure.[13]

My own *Joyce Between Freud and Jung* focuses primarily on a mental process in the minds of the characters which takes the form of a continuous interaction between opposing forces in all of the works. I see this opposition as expanding from Stephen Dedalus's fear of father and drive toward mother into the opposition between skepticism and myth in Joyce's mind, and this division I see as represented by the conflict between Stephen and Leopold Bloom. I use the theories of Jung, which view the mind as regenerating itself through conflict, to describe the transcendence I find in Joyce's last phase.[14] The idea of covering the range of Joyce's thought by combining Freud with Jung goes back to the classic *Skeleton Key to* Finnegans Wake by Joseph Campbell and Henry Morton Robinson (1944), but I explain how the two theories are related in Joyce.

Another combination of Freud with myth appears in Elliott B. Gose's *The Transformation Process in Joyce's* Ulysses. After a fine treatment of Joyce's use of Giordano Bruno's theory that God is present in the process of transformation in his creatures, Gose explains how the characters and the reader achieve release and regeneration through contact with symbols of transformation which Joyce plants in the text.[15] Thus, he shows how myth implants God in the mind of the work.

Despite some drastic differences, Shechner, Gose, and I have a good deal in common. We all make use of overlaps between the minds of author, character, and text. Our positions may be coordinated with the levels of Joycean mentality by one's recognizing the different areas we emphasize: Joyce's ego went on achieving mastery of a world of fantasy while his impulses (projected in characters) continued to divide him, making it necessary for him to believe in the benevolence of myth that appears as a substructure of his text. He was able to embrace immortality in his last phase by decking it with skeptical defenses. Of course, these functions do not exhaust any level.

The individuality and compatibility of these works spring from the magnitude of Freud's vision, and there are many opportunities for further extensions. For example, D. W. Winnicott's theory of shared space between mother and child as the basis of creativity could be applied to various levels of relationship in Joyce, as could Heinz Kohut's about idealizing and transmuting internalization.[16] Nor does one need a new analysis for a new approach: Meredith Anne Skura's use of the analytic process as a method of knowledge, for example, might be applied to stages of Joyce's development or composition.[17]

But a new factor must interrupt this attempt at a harmonious unfolding. At a distance from these three studies are two based on new French theories. Both of these works mix the ideas of Jacques Lacan with the structuralism and deconstruction to which they are related, and it does not seem that the established framework can accommodate them.

Margot Norris's *The Decentered Universe of* Finnegans Wake uses the model of an empty unconscious over which the structure of language on the preconscious level attempts to impose laws. This follows Lacan's equation of language with the unconscious.[18] Norris shows how the effort of language to assert meaning in the *Wake* keeps defeating itself. Rather than being in the *Wake*, the mind she deals with is in language itself, in fact in all languages. The *Wake* consists of deconstructions of this mind, failures of contact between its elements. Norris discovers important qualities that saturate the *Wake*, such as "the grace . . . of freedom."[19] It may be asked, however, whether she recognizes more than a part of the intelligence that orders the *Wake*.

Colin MacCabe, in *James Joyce and the Revolution of the Word*, starts with the idea that desire, which he sees as connected to mother, must be repressed to create reality. He then examines Joyce's mounting effort through his career to destabilize language in order to liberate the revolutionary maternal force of desire from the paternal strictures of fixed meaning by releasing the shifting of different meanings in each word.[20] MacCabe is penetrating in describing how Joyce uses language, though he is not usually as well-focused as Norris.

Both are brilliant books, and a third could be written on Joyce by use of Lacan's theory of transference. But how do such studies relate to other analytic methods? I do not think that the application of Freud to linguistics will replace Freud any more than his social writings replaced his works on the mind. If one locates mind in language, as Joyce did through the image of the letter in the *Wake*, it nevertheless remains mind. And all scientific systems for explaining the motivation of the mind in depth are derived from Freud's.

In Norris, MacCabe, and Lacan, language is troubled by a disturbing undercurrent called guilt or desire. This indicates the extent to which the Freudian mind has here been transplanted to language, and Lacan insists that his theories are implicit in Freud. It remains to be seen to what extent linguistic theories of the mind will prove more viable than Freudian theory or change its main models. But even if all the mental content of Joyce appears through language, we have to consider that deconstruction is only one aspect of language, an aspect that can be used to demolish theories, but not to support life. The constructive aspect prior to deconstruction includes elements that are not conscious, elements of the drive toward life. Freud used these when he found unconscious libidinal meanings in words. An aggregate of these elements, personality, is vital to Joyce, yet it is excluded by deconstruction.

MacCabe says biography must be omitted from consideration in analysis of a text. But he later says that because every text is formed by interaction with other texts, nothing is outside the text, and therefore "the division between author and text cannot be sustained." [21] He admits Joyce as a text, but does not say how this text can be composed without reference to biography. In fact, both MacCabe and Norris describe policies of liberation based partly on Joyce's nonfictional statements. To omit the correspondence between author, text, and reader is to omit communication.

In *The Interpretation of Dreams* Freud says, "it can of course only be the poet's own mind which confronts us in Hamlet." [22] Stephen agrees when he says Shakespeare is "heard" in Hamlet, "the son consubstantial with the father" (*U* 197). They both follow Aristotle: "from art proceed the things of which the form is in the soul of the artist." [23] The individual mind of the author, which is analogous to one volume in the library of the whole language, is the most specific source for the mental content of the work on all levels. This unique construct selects the interferences that make up the deconstruction of language, a deconstruction which is always shaped by individual neurosis. Think of Robbe-Grillet, who set out to write a literature without imposition and proceeded to create a pageant of obsession. In the case of Joyce the ironic displacements of deconstruction are not only critical, but defensive: they allow him to unleash the vital affirmation of the last phase.

How important Joyce's mind is to reading his work is suggested in the *Wake:* "the melos yields the mode and the mode the manners. . . ." (*FW* 57.2–3). Roland McHugh informs us that this refers to the stages of Confucius's learning of the zither: first he learned the melody, then the rhythm, then the mood, and finally "'the kind of man who composed the music. Now I know who he was . . . his eyes when they looked into the distance had the calm gaze of a sheep.'"[24]

This matches other passages in Joyce that indicate not only that artistic creation is personal reproduction, but that the final goal of aesthetic perception, the whatness or soul of the object, is defined by the author's mind. A well-known example is the description of Shem that says that if one peers through the mess of mottage, "the breakages, upheavals distortions, inversions of all this chambermade music one stands, given a grain of goodwill, a fair chance of actually seeing the whirling dervish . . . writing the mystery of himsel. . ." (FW 184.3–10).

This personal depth Joyce refers to continually as the source and goal of art is a principle we use constantly when reading. We could not identify the Confucius quote that provides one of the main meanings of Joyce's line above without knowing Joyce's reading, a biographical fact. Joyce's mind, his structure of associations and impulses, is a substratum of every line of the Wake, the principle that organizes its levels of meanings.

The chief obstacle in literary thought to seeing the mind of an author in his work is the theory of intentional fallacy. This idea is valuable as a warning against applying an author's statement to his work where it does not fit, but it is misused to separate an author's thought from his work absolutely—as if the mind did not control the hand because the hand does not always do what the mind wants. Intention is always essentially related to text. If the author's ideas enter his creation distorted, reversed or even indirectly, the method that can explain the transformation between mind and work is psychoanalysis.

The common origin of every part of the mental structure of the work in a unique personality is invaluable to the critic, but it does not make all parts subject to the same laws. What I have said about the relation of Lacan and deconstruction to psychoanalysis confirms the earlier suggestion that different schools tend to cover different areas of the entire structure. Various levels and connections in various works will emphasize factors accessible to different theories.

This does not mean that all theories are equally valuable. Their value continues to be determined by how well they cover the material—as well as by their consistency and their relation to the major features of depth psychology. Norris's larger sense of context allows her theory to cover the *Wake* better than MacCabe covers the works he writes about, but his greater knowledge of language allows him to develop Joyce's linguistic techniques more extensively than she. Both theories describe impulses that cannot exist without something larger to contain their deconstruction.

Critics, then, should avoid the idea that there is one correct theory for psychologically interpreting literature or even one work. Whatever external authority a theory may have, it must be understood in terms of what function of the work it describes. Norris, for example, remembers the affirmative, mythic view taken by the *Skeleton Key* and shapes her theory to meet this Jungian view. Recognition of how the minds in the text are divided must be accompanied, to avoid fragmentary theories, by an awareness of how they operate as parts of a dynamic mental unity.

Joyce's canon is one continuous expansion of the concept of mind, which grows more powerful and complex from work to work and within each work. *Dubliners* shows a group of minds controlled by society, not suggesting any possibility of freedom until its last story. *A Portrait* shows a young man growing aware of such control and using his knowledge to develop an individual mind. In *Ulysses*, two people come into contact with a mind that unites them, an extra-individual or multi-personal mind. And this dual mind becomes a trinity at the end when Molly Bloom reveals herself as the spirit underlying and proceeding from their relationship. The *Wake*, which is a dream, takes place within the mind, in a world whose shifting characters are mental impulses. The five archetypal figures of the eternal family in the *Wake* embody the interacting parts of a universal mind. The relationship of the parts of this, Joyce's most highly developed psychic apparatus, is examined by Margaret Solomon in *Eternal Geomater*.[25] The Joycean mind thus progresses from a naturalistic nullity to a unity to a duality to a trinity to a quaternity to a quincunx. This multiplication of integrated mental systems was intended by Joyce to express for humanity the maximum possible richness of being. In the depths of this elaboration we can find new principles of mental life and a new understanding of how these principles work together—if we have the flexibility to use every available psychological resource toward the construction of a true Joycean psychology.

Notes

1. (Pittsburgh: Univ. of Pittsburgh Pr., 1973), pp. 200–1, 214–15. A more limited use of statistics is John B. Smith, *Imagery and the Mind of Stephen Dedalus: A Computer-Assisted Study of Joyce's* A Portrait of the Artist as a Young Man (Lewisburg, Pa.: Bucknell Univ. Pr., 1980). Limitations of space oblige me to omit several books that derive Joyce's psychology from his sources, but do not enter into the theoretical questions I am concerned with.

2. *Gödel, Escher, Bach: An Eternal Golden Braid* (New York: Basic Books, 1979); note also Hofstadter and Daniel C. Dennett, *The Mind's I* (New York: Basic Books, 1981).

3. *The Origin of Consciousness in the Breakdown of the Bicameral Mind* (Boston: Houghton Mifflin, 1977).

4. A useful summary of Piaget's vast work is Piaget and Bärbel Inhelder, *The Psychology of the Child*, trans. Helen Weaver (New York: Basic Books, 1969).

5. "Freud and Literature," in *The Liberal Imagination: Essays on Literature and Society* (New York: Anchor Books, 1953), p. 38.

6. *Joyce's* Ulysses *Notesheets in the British Museum*, ed. Phillip F. Herring (Charlottesville: Univ. Pr. of Virginia, 1972), p. 101.

7. Ed. Clive Hart (New York: Barnes and Noble, 1974), p. 74.

8. (New York: Oxford, 1977), p. 54.

9. "Leopold Bloom as Dr. Sigmund Freud," *Mosaic*, 6 (Fall 1972), 23–43.

10. Finnegans Wake: *A Facsimile of Buffalo Notebooks VI.B. 17–20*, ed. David Hayman, James Joyce Archive, v.[33] (New York: Garland, 1978), p. 258. Hayman points out this passage in his Preface to Notebook VI.B.19.

11. Kenner, Ulysses (London: George Allen and Unwin, 1980), p. 112. Kenner credits Bruce Kawin with the idea of the mind of the text. It is a good idea insofar as

it allows us to see the presence of mind on this level, but I hope it will not be used to reduce the fullness of the dynamic concept of mind to a verbal configuration.

12. See Norman N. Holland, *5 Readers Reading* (New Haven: Yale Univ. Pr., 1975).

13. *Joyce in Nighttown: A Psychoanalytic Inquiry into* Ulysses (Berkeley: Univ. of California Pr., 1974).

14. (Port Washington, N.Y.: Kennikat, 1980).

15. (Toronto and Buffalo: Univ. of Toronto Pr., 1980). Psychoanalysis is subordinate to myth in Gose, as it is in the *Skeleton Key*.

16. D. W. Winnicott, *Playing and Reality* (Harmondsworth: Penguin, 1974); Heinz Kohut, *The Analysis of the Self: A Systematic Approach to the Psychoanalytic Treatment of Narcissistic Personality Disorders*, Psychoanalytic Study of the Child, Monograph No. 4 (New York: International Universities Pr., 1971).

17. *The Literary Use of the Psychoanalytic Process* (New Haven: Yale Univ. Pr., 1981).

18. *The Decentered Universe of* Finnegans Wake*: A Structuralist Analysis* (Baltimore, Md.: Johns Hopkins Univ. Pr., 1976). See Jacques Lacan, "The Agency of the Letter in the Unconscious, or Reason since Freud," in *Écrits: A Selection*, trans. Alan Sheridan (New York: Norton, 1977), pp. 146–75.

19. Norris, p. 71.

20. (London: Macmillan, 1979). In addition to Lacan, MacCabe uses Jacques Derrida, whose "Freud and the Scene of Writing," in *Writing and Difference*, trans. Alan Bass (Chicago: Univ. of Chicago Pr., 1978), pp. 196–231, should be read by all psycho-critics.

21. MacCabe, pp. 85, 115.

22. *The Interpretation of Dreams* (First Part), *The Standard Edition of the Complete Psychological Works of Sigmund Freud*, trans. and ed. James Strachey in collaboration with Anna Freud, assisted by Alix Strachey and Alan Tyson (London: Hogarth, 1953, 1958), IV, 265.

23. *Metaphysics*, 1032b, *The Basic Works of Aristotle*, ed. Richard McKeon (New York: Random House, 1941), p. 792.

24. *Annotations to* Finnegans Wake (Baltimore: Johns Hopkins Univ. Pr., 1980), p. 57.

25. *Eternal Geomater: The Sexual Universe of* Finnegans Wake (Carbondale: Southern Illinois Univ. Pr., 1969). Another striking treatment of the psychological interactions of the *Wake* is Randolph Splitter, "The Sane and Joyful Spirit," *James Joyce Quarterly*, 13 (Spring 1976), 350–65.

9

SUZETTE A. HENKE

James Joyce and Women: The Matriarchal Muse

James Joyce could hardly be considered a feminist author. As a young man, he often made fun of the "new woman" seeking social and economic independence at the end of the nineteenth century. He took a bemused attitude toward Francis Sheehy-Skeffington's passionate defense of women's rights. And his own relationship with Nora Barnacle swerved erratically between sexual obsession and filial dependence. "I wonder is there some madness in me," Joyce wrote to Nora. "Or is love madness? One moment I see you like a virgin or madonna the next moment I see you shameless, insolent, half-naked and obscene" (L II, 243).

And yet it would be a mistake to identify Joyce with his misogynist alter-ego, Stephen Dedalus. In a conversation with Arthur Power, the mature Joyce championed the contemporary "revolt of women against the idea that they are the mere instruments of men." He defended the "emancipation of women" as "the greatest revolution in our time in the most important relationship there is—that between men and women."[1]

Joyce's own attitude toward women always remained highly ambivalent. The dichotomy in Joyce's mind was not, apparently, between virgin and whore, but between narcissistic virgin and phallic mother—between the untouched and untouchable ingénue and the experienced maternal female. In the guise of a Dublin coquette, the Virgin Mary of Catholicism became for Joyce a nubile temptress, coyly flirting with adult sexuality. At the same time, Joyce was fascinated by the Circean image of a dangerous, threatening "phallic mother"—an omnipotent female who could nurture or destroy the male enthralled by her charms.

For Joyce, woman is, first and foremost, a figure of motherhood. "*Amor matris*, subjective and objective genitive, may be the only true thing in life" (*U* 207). Woman emerges in his work as virgin or whore, but usually within the context of maternity. The mother is a figure of material immanence, bound to mortality through the navelcord of physiological process. And the temptress is portrayed, more often than not, as a "potential mother" in training. Compelled by the life-force of the species, she becomes a pawn to the instinctual drives of racial propagation. From her Oedipal role as "Papa's little bedpal. Lump of love" (*U* 39), the adolescent girl learns narcissistic tricks to tempt the ingenuous suitor. Her body is her sole commodity, the one "good" that she can trade for the infinite security of marriage. Most of Joyce's female characters move from adolescent narcissism to shrewish maternity. All too frequently, their conjugal affiliations prove physically onerous and psychologically diminishing. Unfortunately, Joyce's single women fare little better than their married sisters. The "spinsters" in his fiction look forward to barren lives of isolation, cut off from life's feast of amorous delectation.

Traditionally, readers have either praised Joyce for his intimate knowledge of the female psyche or condemned his view of woman as stereotyped and reductive. Most early criticism focused on the archetypal nature of Joyce's female portraits. Zack Bowen, for instance, found in the poems of *Chamber Music* a paradigm of Joyce's "eternal feminine." The triune woman addressed in the lyrics is a panoply of contradictions—"virgin and temptress, creator and destroyer, prisoner and jailer, a source of fulfillment and a source of denial." This "goldenhaired" image, Bowen tells us, serves as a prototype for the "ambiguous, everchanging, multiform montage of womankind" later revealed in Joyce's work.[2]

It is not a very great leap from a celebration of the feminine archetype to a denigration of the female stereotype. As Simone de Beauvoir reminds us, the idealization of woman as goddess can be just as debasing as a negative representation: "To say that Woman is Flesh, to say that the Flesh is Night and Death, or that it is the splendor of the Cosmos, is to abandon terrestrial truth. . . . Woman is not merely a carnal object. . . . To assimilate her to Nature is simply to act from prejudice."[3] Feminist critics who object to Joyce's writing often attack the archetypal dimensions of his female portraits. Kate Millett, who devotes a chapter of *Sexual Politics* to a critique of D. H. Lawrence, mentions Joyce only in passing, as an author "fond of presenting woman as 'nature,' 'unspoiled primeval understanding,' and the 'eternal feminine.'"[4] Annis Pratt, who is willing to acknowledge Joyce's literary genius, nevertheless remarks that "it is difficult not to feel about Molly Bloom on her chamberpot what Eldridge Cleaver must feel about Jack Benny's Rochester."[5]

There is, however, another side to Joyce's writing—a more ironic and compassionate dimension evident to the reader who applies a judicious, "parallactic" perspective to the canon. Joyce clearly eschews the literary fraternity that Shulamith Firestone describes as "Virility, Inc." As early as *Dubliners*, he emerges as a revisionist thinker determined to see old institutions in a new light and to question traditional patterns of social organization. He openly challenges an authoritarian power structure and draws acerbic caricatures of masculine bravado. By comically deflating prevalent stereotypes of male prowess and female passivity, Joyce advocates a more enlightened ideal of androgynous behavior for both sexes.

In *Dubliners*, Joyce portrays a society radically torn between sentimentality and squalor, with female characters at the focal point of this caustic, multi-dimensional mimesis. Women provide a translucent screen on which men act out melodramatic scripts or engage in bizarre, narcissistic behavior. Many of the stories reiterate the theme of patriarchal futility. The males of Dublin struggle to defend the law and the word, though reason and logic founder in sentimental drunkenness. The women of *Dubliners*, even more than the men, are clearly depicted as societal victims. Female characters are condemned to involuntary celibacy by their own timidity and fear, or to loveless marriages and altruistic motherhood. Subservient to fathers and patriarchal husbands, they vent their anger through shrewish and manipulative practices. In a land of decay, women are the natural victims of authoritarian abuse, and children become emotional casualties of adult frustration. All too often, critics have maligned, misapprehended, or simply ignored the women of *Dubliners*. In "*Dubliners*: Women in Irish Society," Florence Walzl attempts to redress the balance by examining some of the gender attributions operative in late nineteenth-century Ireland.[6] Edward Brandabur, in *A Scrupulous Meanness*, offers a detailed psychoanalytic study of the individual stories and provides a lucid analysis of sexual repression.[7]

The women characters in *Stephen Hero* and *A Portrait of the Artist* are thinly sketched and fairly two-dimensional. Seen through the eyes of a self-consciously rebellious young man, females are perceived as threatening or enchanting, seductive or aloof. Their demeanor is largely contingent on Stephen's adolescent attitude and misogynist frame of mind. Joyce's notes for *Stephen Hero* suggest that the protagonist feels a need "to avenge himself on Irish women who, he says, are the cause of all the moral suicide in the island" (*SH* 200). The shadowy Mercedes of *A Portrait* becomes the romantic object of Stephen's prepubescent fantasies, just as the Virgin Mary later appeals to his ascetic, "monkish" mentality. Once at university, the more sophisticated Stephen rejects Irish puritanism and the sexual mores of bourgeois society. In *Stephen Hero*, he proposes to the ingenuous Emma that they "live one night together," then "say goodbye in the morning . . . never to see each other again!" (*SH* 198). Understandably shocked, Emma dismisses her bohemian suitor as an incipient madman. Stephen, in turn, rationalizes his rejection "by anathemising . . . Emma as the most deceptive and cowardly of marsupials" (*SH* 210).[8]

Both *Stephen Hero* and *Portrait* might be seen as extended delineations of Stephen's "flight from woman," first in the guise of a maternal authority figure, then as a Circean temptress.[9] Like Schopenhauer, Stephen devises "a theory of dualism which would symbolise the twin eternities of spirit and nature in the twin eternities of male and female" (*SH* 210). He sees women as emblems of the flesh allied with the chaos of nature. Terrified of the "eternal temptress," and haunted by fears of erotic compulsion, Stephen seeks Freudian mastery through the "spiritual-heroic refrigerating apparatus, invented and patented in all countries by Dante Alighieri" (*P* 252). The poet can control the vagaries of sexual excitation by banishing the temptress to a refrigerated world of aesthetic stasis. The creative process functions as an exercise in emotional compensation: it allows Stephen to "transubstantiate" the female into an accessible *objet d'art*.

The temptress of Stephen's villanelle in chapter five is most likely a further projection of E—— C—— in still another poetic emanation.[10] The young woman whose "strange and wilful heart" eludes the suffering Stephen is here celebrated as a voluptuous muse— naked, yielding, "odorous and lavish-limbed," possessed in a moment of aesthetic ecstasy. Emma merges with all the sirens and beautiful women of religious history and myth—with the Virgin Mary, Dante's Beatrice, and Yeats's "secret rose." As seductress and autoerotic muse, she offers the poet both sensuous and imaginative satisfaction.

Throughout *A Portrait*, Joyce appears to be satirizing Stephen's brash misogyny as a dimension of adolescent narcissism. The young man's fear of woman and his flight from the "eternal feminine" are factors that inhibit his artistic growth. Before Stephen can become a true priest of the imagination, he must first allow his consciousness to be "feminized." He must incorporate the *anima*—the fluid, fertile, feminine principle—into the logocentric domain of his art.

Richard Rowan, the protagonist of Joyce's *Exiles*, shares some of Stephen's misogynist propensities. Joyce warns us in a note that "Richard must not appear as a champion of woman's rights. His language at times must be nearer to that of Schopenhauer against women and he must show at times a deep contempt for the long-haired, short-legged sex" (*E* 120). In *Exiles*, all the world is a stage, and Richard Rowan assumes the role of author-director in the drama of his own betrayal. Horrified by the prospect of cuckoldry, he wants to plunge into the void of incertitude and "freely" offer his common-law wife Bertha to her suitor Robert Hand. Like Kierkegaard,

Richard defines ultimate spiritual possession as an act of sacrificial generosity. Voluntary renunciation frees the individual from the ponderous burden of jealousy and desire. Having choreographed the scene of erotic temptation for Bertha and Robert, Richard may then withdraw, like the god of creation, "within or behind or beyond or above his handiwork" and remain indifferent, "paring his fingernails" (P 215). Paradoxically, Richard plays the benevolent patriarch by assuming that Bertha is a conjugal possession; he takes for granted that she is *his* to give away, like a cow or a piece of movable property. Hence the irony of Richard's parabolic lesson to his son Archie: "While you have a thing it can be taken from you," he tells Archie. "But when you give it, you have given it. No robber can take it from you. . . . It is yours then for ever. . . . It will be yours always" (E 46–47). Bertha, evidently, is the "thing" in question, and Robert the potential robber.

Bertha, to her credit, maintains a combination of dignity and naturalness throughout the play. She instinctively penetrates the convoluted psychodynamics of Richard's manipulation. "For your own sake you urged me to it," she accuses. "To be free yourself" (E 103). In a conversation with Beatrice, Bertha angrily dismisses the false world of "ideas and ideas" (E 100). "Do you think I am a stone?" she asks bitterly. "I am very proud of myself, if you want to know. . . . And you . . . will never humble me, any of you" (E 100). Reversing the Pygmalion/Galatea relationship earlier envisaged by Robert, Bertha claims with fierce, maternal pride that it is she who made Richard "a man" (E 100). Through love and amorous devotion, she has spiritually given birth to the mature artist who will, in turn, conceive and give birth to poetic ideas. At this point in the drama, Bertha proves to be a fiery, passionate heroine, independent and free. In her own right, she asserts a creative liberty that transcends the sexual imbroglio engineered by Richard.

Bertha emerges as the "heroine" of Joyce's Ibsenian drama. Until recently, however, few critics have acknowledged the centrality of her role in the play.[11] Most scholars have focused attention on Richard, whom Ellmann describes as a "metaphysical victor."[12]

William York Tindall bluntly dismisses Bertha as Richard's "stooge," a woman who gullibly cooperates in her own victimization. Carole Brown and Leo Knuth share Tindall's acerbity when they describe Bertha as "little more than a psychological satellite," "annoyingly imperceptive," and "neither emphatic nor discerning." And Hugh Kenner, who reads the entire play as an exercise in Joycean irony, sees Bertha as a neurotic "parody of the exiled Eve."[13]

It is not surprising that so many critics have responded to the protean portrait of Joyce's heroine and to the dramatic ambiguity of *Exiles* with some doubt and a great deal of skepticism. Doubt, Joyce would tell us, "is the thing. Life is suspended in doubt like the world in the void. You might find this in some sense treated in *Exiles*."[14]

From the very beginning of *Ulysses*, Molly Bloom emerges as the *clou* of Joyce's novel—the key to the male-dominated, anti-heroic modern epic, and the nail in the coffin of bourgeois, sentimental literature. Her world view is gynocentric, and her monologue "turns like the huge earth ball slowly surely and evenly round and round spinning, its four cardinal points being the female breasts, arse, womb and [cunt] expressed by the words *because, bottom, . . . woman, yes*" (*L* I, 170).

Molly is both mother and lover to Leopold Bloom, whose infantile desires for maternal domination clothe themselves in sado-masochistic, Circean reverie. Other women in the novel are either forebears, extensions, or pale shadows of Joyce's modern Penelope. When Bloom takes a polymorphously perverse delight in imagining an affair with the "nextdoor girl," his daydream suggests a younger, more vivacious Molly—the kind of woman who would not hesitate to flagellate a miscreant spouse. Bloom thrills at the voyeuristic image of a woman's ankle and takes masturbatory pleasure from the sight of Gerty MacDowell's transparent stockings. A fetish for legs, ankles, stockings, and hats displaces a more focused desire for Molly's "peachy" thighs and for the vestigial phallus ascribed to the powerful, authoritative female. When Bloom plays the transvestite, he is, in fact, offering himself in fantasies of abasement before Molly as voluptuous matriarch. Molly Bloom is metamorphosed in her husband's erotic imagination into the threatening figure of Bella/ Bello, a castrating whoremistress who punishes and emasculates. Bella represents the phallic mother *par excellence*—a vampiric woman who seduces and devours her timorous mates. Preying on the "beastly" sensuality of the male, this surrealistic Circe exposes the nightmare underside of lascivious fantasy.

Since the publication of *Ulysses* in 1922, readers have seen Molly either as an archetypal representation of Joyce's "eternal feminine" or as a debased stereotype of female eroticism. Carl Jung, for instance, praised Joyce for revealing a dimension of female psychology heretofore obscured in psychoanalysis. He described the "Penelope" episode of *Ulysses* as a "string of veritable psychological peaches. I suppose the devil's grandmother knows so much about the real psychology of a woman. I didn't" (*L* III, 253). Philip Toynbee qualified Jung's assertion by suggesting that Molly represents not the "female mind" but "the *anima*, the female image in the mind of the male, sensual, intuitive, submarine." [15]

Readers have invariably projected onto Joyce's Penelope an image cast in the mold of their own experiences. Thus, to a woman of Mary Colum's generation schooled in the values of Catholic Ireland, Molly seemed to exhibit all the sensitivity of one of the greater apes. Writing in 1922, Colum interpreted the Penelope episode as a kind of zoological experiment, "an exhibition of the mind of a female gorilla who has been corrupted by contact with humans." [16]

Molly's omnivorous sexual appetites, prolific fantasies, adulterous activities, and verbal frankness have all contributed to the creation of a negative stereotype. J. Mitchell Morse dismisses Molly as a "dirty joke," an earth-goddess who sneers at fecundity. The Penelope episode, he tells us, "is the bitterest and deadliest thing Joyce ever wrote." [17] Darcy O'Brien finds Molly overwhelmingly narcissistic, a "comic example of a self-loving woman," who "would devour any man." He is appalled by the crudity of her language and insists that "for all of her fleshly charms and engaging bravado, she is at heart a thirty-shilling whore." [18] In a recent *Harper's* article on

"Joyce and Nora," Edna O'Brien makes similar remarks with a strikingly different emphasis. She praises Molly as "a marvel of licentiousness, noddle, and nonguilt." O'Brien is delighted that Joyce's heroine "remembers the celebration of her own body, and the sure knowledge of her prowess with the opposite sex and her own unconditional surrender, which is inextricably bound up with the image of the crushed flower and the image of nature and of the sea giving forth all that it has."[19]

As David Hayman points out, Molly tends to reflect the sum of the "attitudes we accumulate toward her." We cannot define her simply as an archetypal "Gea-Tellus," or as a stereotypical "Great Whore." Hayman marshals convincing evidence that Molly has been technically faithful to Bloom for the past ten and a half years, and that Boylan is her first and only extramarital lover. "Critics in general," he observes, "are prone to exaggerate Molly's sexual vitality, her seductive charms, and her lewdness."[20]

Few readers have dealt with Molly as a realistic character—a turn-of-the-century Dublin matron whose feminine resources are dwindling, and who desperately needs the kind of verification provided by male approval.[21] Although Molly is a music-hall *artiste*, most of her energies are directed toward sexual projects. She seems to have internalized the male-created image of woman as eternal temptress. Molly spends her time devising amorous schemes, most of which remain on the level of fantasy or flirtation. Her love affair with Boylan is only partially and temporarily satisfying. It unleashes a torrent of erotic possibilities in Molly's imagination, as she fantasizes encounters with the poet Stephen Dedalus, naked young boys, "a sailor off the sea thatd be hot on for it . . . or one of those wildlooking gipsies in Rathfarnham . . . or a murderer anybody" (*U* 777).

One of the principal motivations for Molly's affair with Boylan seems to be the threat of diminishing sexual power. Raised by a military father in a male-dominated atmosphere, Molly believes in traditional sex roles. Convinced that a woman can act only by influencing men, she is afraid of being "all washed up" by the age of thirty-five and exhibits a growing fear of sexual obsolescence. "As for being a woman," she reflects pessimistically, "as soon as youre old they might as well throw you out in the bottom of the ash pit" (*U* 759). No wonder Molly feels obsessively attracted to Boylan. After a decade of sexual abstinence, she longs for reassurance that she is not yet "finished out and laid on the shelf" (*U* 766).

Trapped in narrow, restrictive "feminine" roles, Molly may act the part of a sedate matron or a lascivious vamp. In either case, however, she has little opportunity to take charge of her life. Molly lies in bed, reads salacious novels, digests pears and potted meat, and sometimes sings; she occasionally cleans house, shops for stockings, or moves furniture.[22] The resumption of an interrupted musical career, along with the delights of rehearsals with her organizer/manager Boylan, provides an unusual opportunity for distraction in a tedious domestic routine.

Molly's great talent, apparently, is neither song nor sex, but dream and amorous reverie. She is, in her own right, a poet of the imagination whose final soliloquy elevates *Ulysses* to the heights of lyrical discourse. By virtue of her capacious, flowing monologue, Molly moves in the direction of archetypal eloquence. Her erotic preoccupations convince us of a fertile, feminine imagination creating a web of artistry from the quotidian concerns of female life. On various levels, Molly can be envisaged as both goddess and whore, Dublin housewife and phallic mother. She is precursor to Anna Livia Plurabelle, the great mother/lover portrayed in *Finnegans Wake*.

Joyce himself expresses admiration for the "penelopean patience" (*FW* 123.4–5) of Molly Bloom and, with "labiolingual . . . tongue in . . . cheek" (*FW* 122.32–34), makes fun of the reader of *Ulysses* who struggles, out of salacious interest, through "a colophon of no fewer than seven hundred and thirtytwo strokes tailed by a leaping lasso" (*FW* 123.5–6). Somewhat abashedly, Joyce satirizes both the pornographic prurience of his audience and his own authorial control when he asks: "who thus at all this marvelling but will press on hotly to see the vaulting feminine libido of those interbranching ogham sex upandinsweeps sternly controlled and easily repersuaded by the uniform matteroffactness of a meandering male fist?" (*FW* 123.7–10).

Nowhere is Joyce's anti-patriarchal obsession more evident than in *Finnegans Wake*. If there is to be a feminist re-evaluation of Joyce's work, it will probably lie in the direction of a post-structuralist, semiotic analysis of this most radical and deracinated of texts. Julia Kristeva, for instance, praises *Finnegans Wake* for challenging paternal authority "not only ideologically, but in the workings of language itself, by a return to semiotic rhythms connotatively maternal."[23] Kristeva associates Joyce with the "cult of the mother" characteristic of oriental religions. The state, the family, and Catholicism are the sacrosanct institutions he sets out to "deconstruct" through a work of literary subversion. Kristeva argues that in the *Wake* Joyce attacks the ideological code of patriarchy embodied in domestic, religious, and political myths, as much as he subverts the linguistic code basic to a logocentric culture.[24]

In all his work, Joyce suggests that human civilization progresses through a continual dialectic between Logos and Eros, between male and female principles, between symbolic discourse and semiotic process. Women represent for him the opulence, the chaos, and the "naturalness" of passion, in opposition to the masculine impulse toward domination and control. In *Finnegans Wake*, the earth-mother Gea-Tellus has given way to the more primal forces of flowing water, symbolic of a mysterious, protean unconscious. Anna Livia Plurabelle emerges as Joyce's "allincluding, most farraginous" archetype. As mother and lover of men and women, she freely flows into the lap of "Old Father Ocean," the watery tomb of death and resurrection. In the persona of ALP, womb flows into tomb, to continue the endless process of evaporation and vaporous redistribution that characterizes cosmic regeneration. As womb of the world, Anna Livia absorbs both squalor and sentiment, reality and dream. She is the archetypal river-woman, flowing out of the depths, and carrying the leaves, flowers, and sediment of life in the wake of her shifting shoreline. Whereas the principal male persona, Humphrey Chimpden Earwicker, is identified in terms of an ancient Irish giant, buried in the rocks of Howth and Chapelizod, Anna Livia embodies a fluid, semiotic, ever-elusive reality. She captures the Heraclitean flux that fascinated her creator, and she forever changes in the context of a changeless biological cycle.[25]

In *Finnegans Wake*, the obsessive, logocentric reality of the male, along with the *idée-fixe* of patriarchal authority, has been ossified into stony impotence. The compulsive desire for mastery has hardened into the rocky sensibility of Finn MacCool, an Irish giant helplessly shaking a "meandering male fist." The masculine persona is paralyzed in intractable patriarchy. The female, in contrast, remains fluid and free. The traditional hero, dead and outmoded from the beginning of the book, has to be dreamed into waking, into "array surrection" by Anna's life-giving riverrun.[26]

For Joyce, the dream of male authority has degenerated into the nightmare conflict enacted by Shem and Shaun, the primitive Mutt and Jute, and the adversaries Mercius and Justius. Locked in endless civil war, the sons triumph over their moribund progenitor, but appropriate his authority with little cognizance of the destruction they perpetuate. Trapped in patterns of meaningless violence, the brothers find solace in the maternal sanctuary provided by ALP.

Anna's daughter Issy is portrayed as a flirtatious ingénue, stuttering through a narcissistic dream of prelapsarian innocence.[27] Vainly staring into her mirror and enumerating her adolescent charms, Issy learns to tempt and to please, to smile and to win male approval. She is beginning to master the various feminine roles that will make her attractive as an adult. Issy idly polishes her skill in politesse, with the same care that she polishes her mirror. The letters she writes, like her mirror, reflect a dazzling self-image. In contrast to Issy, Anna Livia has survived and transcended the female roles ascribed to her by traditional society. Even more than Molly Bloom, ALP captures the rhythms of the capacious unconscious. She is open, fluid, and forever "yea-saying" to the rushing torrent of temporal phenomena that characterizes the "given" moment of cosmic experience.[28]

Biographical evidence suggests that Joyce eventually came to terms with the kind of adolescent misogyny exhibited by his fictional persona, Stephen Dedalus. Through Nora Barnacle, Joyce found the madonna and muse who could both inspire his art and satisfy his sexual desires. Nora was the fluid, fertile woman whose yea-saying sexuality finally released the inhibitions, both artistic and sexual, that once had stifled her shy but willing son-lover, "Jimmy Joyce." In an amorous invocation, Joyce wrote to his wife: "Guide me, my saint, my angel, Lead me forward. *Everything* that is noble and exalted and deep and true and moving in what I write comes, I believe, from you. O take me into your soul of souls and then I will become indeed the poet of my race" (*L* II, 248).

Notes

1. Arthur Power, *Conversations with James Joyce*, ed. Clive Hart (New York: Barnes and Noble, 1974), p. 35.

2. Zack Bowen, "Goldenhair: Joyce's Archetypal Female," *Literature and Psychology*, 17 (1967), 219, 227. For a more recent discussion of this lyrical prototype, see Robert Boyle's essay on "The Woman Hidden in *Chamber Music*," in *Women in Joyce*, ed. Suzette Henke and Elaine Unkeless (Urbana: Univ. of Illinois Pr., 1982), pp. 3–30.

3. Simone de Beauvoir, *The Second Sex*, trans. and ed. H. M. Parshley (New York: Knopf, 1952), p. 255.

4. Kate Millett, *Sexual Politics* (Garden City, N.Y.: Doubleday, 1970), p. 285.

5. Annis Pratt, "The New Feminist Criticism," *College English*, 32 (1971), 877.

6. Florence Walzl, "*Dubliners*: Women in Irish Society," in *Women in Joyce*, pp. 31–56.

7. Edward Brandabur, *A Scrupulous Meanness* (Urbana: Univ. of Illinois Pr., 1971). In an article of this scope, my discussion of critical response to Joyce's women cannot, of course, be exhaustive. For a survey of past criticism, see Marvin Magalaner and Richard M. Kain, *Joyce: The Man, the Work, the Reputation* (1956; rpt. New York: Collier Books, 1962) and Thomas F. Staley, "James Joyce," in *Anglo-Irish Literature: A Review of Research*, ed. Richard J. Finneran (New York: Modern Language Association of America, 1976), pp. 366–435.

8. For further discussion, see Bonnie Scott's recent article "Emma Clery in *Stephen Hero*," in *Women in Joyce*, pp. 57–81.

9. See Suzette Henke, "Stephen Dedalus and Women: A Portrait of the Artist as a Young Misogynist," in *Women in Joyce*, pp. 82–107. Sheldon R. Brivic offers an extensive discussion of the Oedipal complexities in *Portrait* in the first section of *Joyce between Freud and Jung* (Port Washington, N.Y.: Kennikat, 1980). See also Mark Shechner, "The Song of the Wandering Aengus: James Joyce and His

Mother," in Ulysses: *Fifty Years*, ed. Thomas F. Staley (Bloomington: Indiana Univ. Pr., 1974) and Hélène Cixous, *The Exile of James Joyce*, trans. Sally Purcell (New York: David Lewis, 1972). Chester G. Anderson gives us an excellent psychoanalytic study in "Baby Tuckoo: Joyce's 'Features of Infancy,'" in *Approaches to Joyce's Portrait*, ed. Thomas F. Staley and Bernard Benstock (Pittsburgh: Univ. of Pittsburgh Pr., 1976), pp. 135–69.

10. For further discussion, see Robert Scholes, "Stephen Dedalus, Poet or Esthete?" *PMLA*, 89 (1964), 484–89.

11. Ruth Bauerle, in a recent essay on "Bertha's Role in *Exiles*," offers convincing evidence that Bertha is the dominating figure in the drama (*Women in Joyce*, pp. 108–31).

12. *James Joyce* (New York: Oxford Univ. Pr., 1959), p. 366.

13. William York Tindall, *A Reader's Guide to James Joyce* (New York: Farrar, 1959), p. 111. Carole Brown and Leo Knuth, "James Joyce's *Exiles*: The Ordeal of Richard Rowan," *James Joyce Quarterly*, 17 (1979), 16. Hugh Kenner, *Dublin's Joyce* (Bloomington: Indiana Univ. Pr., 1956), p. 89.

14. Ellmann, p. 568.

15. Philip Toynbee, "A Study of James Joyce's *Ulysses*," in *James Joyce: Two Decades of Criticism*, ed. Seon Givens (New York: Vanguard, 1948), p. 282.

16. Mary Colum, "The Confessions of James Joyce," in *James Joyce: The Critical Heritage*, ed. Robert H. Deming (London: Routledge & Kegan Paul, 1970), I, 233.

17. J. Mitchell Morse, "Molly Bloom Revisited," in *A James Joyce Miscellany*, Second Series, ed. Marvin Magalaner (Carbondale: Southern Illinois Univ. Pr., 1959), p. 149.

18. Darcy O'Brien, *The Conscience of James Joyce* (Princeton: Princeton Univ. Pr., 1968), pp. 204, 207, 211.

19. Edna O'Brien, "Joyce and Nora," *Harper's*, September 1980, p. 71.

20. David Hayman, "The Empirical Molly," in *Approaches to Ulysses*, ed. Thomas F. Staley and Bernard Benstock (Pittsburgh: Univ. of Pittsburgh Pr., 1970), pp. 111, 118.

21. Notable exceptions are David Hayman, in his "The Empirical Molly," and Elaine Unkeless, in "The Conventional Molly Bloom," in *Women in Joyce*, pp. 150–68.

22. The issue of who moved the furniture in the Bloom household, also known as the "Kenner conundrum," has aroused an astonishing amount of critical debate. Hugh Kenner, through circumspect detective work, concluded that Molly was both an inexperienced and unwilling seductress—so shy, in fact, that she stalled for time by asking Boylan to move furniture before making love. ("Molly's Masterstroke," *James Joyce Quarterly*, 10 [1972], 19–28). Bernard Benstock and Margaret Honton have both raised critical objections and defend Molly's word that she herself

moved the furniture. See Bernard Benstock, "The Kenner Conundrum" (*JJQ*, 13 [1976], 428–35). In "Molly's Mistressstroke," Margaret Honton adds a feminist defence of Molly's physical strength and spiritual vitality (*JJQ*, 14 [1976], 25–30).

23. Julia Kristeva, *Polylogue* (Paris: Editions du Seuil, 1977), p. 16. Translation mine.

24. Kristeva, p. 16.

25. For an extended discussion of the persona of ALP, see Margot Norris, "Anna Livia Plurabelle: The Dream Woman," in *Women in Joyce*, pp. 197–213.

26. In 1905 Joyce wrote to his brother Stanislaus on heroism: "I am sure . . . that the whole structure of heroism is, and always was, a damned lie" (*L* II, 81).

27. See Shari Benstock's discussion of Issy's multiple, fragmented personalities in "The Genuine Christine: Psychodynamics of Issy," in *Women in Joyce*, pp. 164–96.

28. Two recent structuralist interpretations have served to reinforce the antipatriarchal dimensions of Joyce's radical linguistic "chaosmos." In *The Decentered Universe of* Finnegans Wake, Margot Norris describes the *Wake* as a literary revolution against the mythic and psychological constraints imposed by patriarchal law (Baltimore, Md.: Johns Hopkins Univ. Pr., 1976). Colin MacCabe similarly speculates in *James Joyce and the Revolution of the Word* that *Finnegans Wake* registers the impact of "female language" on "phallocentric male discourse" (New York: Barnes and Noble, 1979).

10

ROBERT BOYLE, S.J.

Joyce and Faith

". . . if an ear aye sieze"

"Eschatology" is not, to my ear, a pleasant word. The fact that only a tiny exhalation removes it from "scatology" may contribute to my feeling, but I believe that both its clumsy rawness as a recently contrived effort to draw Greek profundity into a theological area and its intimacy with death, judgment, and hell contribute more largely to my distaste (like Father Arnall of *A Portrait*, I omit heaven). Yet it is that word upon which Joyce centers in a passage which for me constitutes his most powerful assertion of his own artistic faith. The first sentence of this climactic passage sets the tone: "He is cured by faith who is sick of fate" (*FW* 482.30–31).

"I have found no man yet with a faith like mine." So the youthful Joyce expressed himself in November 1902 to Lady Gregory, asserting the only religion that, apparently, sustained him throughout his lifelong testing of himself "against the powers, against the world rulers of this present darkness . . ." (Eph. 6:12): "I shall try myself against the powers of the world. All things are inconstant except the faith in the soul, which changes all things and fills their inconstancy with light" (*L* I, 53).

One of the bases upon which Joyce structured his own faith was, in my opinion, the words and example of another rebel against the dominant orthodoxy, who also defied the powers of this world and who found in his own soul the constancy of light and the power to change all things—Paul of Tarsus. I will enlarge upon only one of my several bases for this opinion, Joyce's magnificent act of faith couched in the Cork idiom of his father's dialect: "The prouts who will invent a writing there ultimately is the poeta, still more learned, who discovered the raiding there originally" (*FW* 482.31–33). Only one kind of human being will fulfill the quest for the literary artist's ultimate goal—the poet whose reading will undo the original raiding and whose writing will newly create the old eschatology.

Finnegans Wake, I take it, is Joyce's "book of kills," not only his own personal version of the Christian faith in which he developed as that faith is embodied in the Book of Kells, Ireland's treasured ancient illuminated New Testament barely rescued from ancient raidings, but embodied equally well in the "kil" (Gaelic for "church") of his own body—"he who raised Christ Jesus from the dead will give life to your mortal bodies also through his Spirit which dwells in you" (Rom. 8:11)—the shrine of the fearless soul which set off so bravely to joust with the powers of this world. And this testament of the battle-scarred mature Joyce goes on to express exactly how this ultimate discovery is achieved: "That's the point of eschatology our book of kills reaches for now in soandso many counterpoint words" (*FW* 482.33–34).

Joyce's testament of faith reaches multidirectionally in counterpointed words: compare Stephen's musings on "the slow growth and change of rite and dogma like his own rare thoughts, a chemistry of stars. Symbol of the apostles in the mass for pope Marcellus . . ." (*U* 21). Joyce's interest in Palestrina as musical artificer rises from his conviction that those many-leveled notes, like the many-leveled Catholic rites and dogmas of the faith he was born into, would last like the stars of Stephen's "chemistry of stars" image. Joyce wanted that same immortality for the words which his soul, his imagination, made flesh.

Stephen's judgment on Palestrina's worth finds agreement in current opinion: "Through the works of Giovanni da Palestrina, the model composer of the Catholic Counter-Reformation, Renaissance

modal counterpoint has influenced the teaching of musical composition to this day, suggesting the near perfection with which it conveys some fundamental aspects of the historic European ideal of
composition as the art of lasting musical structures." [1]

In the atmosphere in which Joyce developed, the significance of
"the mass for pope Marcellus" (Stephen's small *p* keeps Marcellus in
his place) was well recognized: "He [St. Charles Borromeo] celebrated a solemn Mass in presence of the pontiff on 19 June, 1565, at
which Palestrina's great 'Missa Papae Marcelli' was sung. These historical data are the only discoverable basis for the legends, so long
repeated by historians, concerning the trial before the cardinals and
pope of the cause of polyphonic music, and its vindication by Palestrina, in the composition and performance of three masses, the
'Missa Papae Marcelli' among them." [2] In that same account, if Joyce
looked at it (as he well may have done), both the similarities and
contrasts to the passionately dedicated young Stephen might have
caught Joyce's attention: "Palestrina's significance lies not so much
in his unprecedented gifts of mind and heart, his creative and constructive powers, as in the fact that he made them the medium for
the expression in tones of the state of his own soul, which, trained
and formed by St. Philip, was attuned to and felt with the
Church." [3]

What Palestrina did with tones Joyce aimed to do with words.
Through polyphonic structuring Joyce plotted to create verbal
beauty in varied and unexpected, uncoded, original times and
spaces. Joyce told Frank Budgen, "In writing the Mass for Pope
Marcellus Palestrina did more than surpass himself as a musician.
With that great effort, consciously made, he saved music for the
Church." [4] In *Finnegans Wake* Joyce surpassed himself as a literary
artist, as his "soandso many counterpoint words" attest.

Notice that Joyce's aim is not "to reach" the point but "to reach
for" the unreachable ultimate; he does not expect to attain it. Here I
find an echo of young Stephen's murmured submission to Mr. Tate at
Belvedere:

—Here. It's about the Creator and the soul. Rrm . . . rrm . . .
rrm. . . . Ah! *without a possibility of ever approaching nearer.* That's heresy.
Stephen murmured:
—I meant *without a possibility of ever reaching.* (P 79)

Even the adolescent Stephen could see, in spite of the humiliation
exacted by a dictatorial teacher, the natural impossibility of a limited creature's reaching (in the sense of comprehending) an infinite
being. The mature Joyce far more fully realized the artist's job of
structuring musical words that forever reach into that infinite void
of mystery—"In the buginning is the woid"—which they can never
encompass—"in the muddle is the sounddance and thereinofter
you're in the unbewised again, vund vulsyvolsy" (*FW* 378.29–31).
Joyce's words make the muddled sounddance, and after the dancers
die away we find ourselves turning and turning still, world without
end. *Finnegans Wake's* verbal rhythms dance in our ears as we plunge
into the timely muddle of many words, and *then* in time and *there* in
space and *often* and *after* (counterpointed into "thereinofter"), we are
back in the mystery of the whirling void again.

We reach for "the point of eschatology." That unlovely word
thrust its pedantic bones into English, according to the *Oxford English Dictionary*, about 1844, under theological auspices. This "science" of the "four last things"—death, judgment, heaven, hell—
apparently emerged from the current intense theological focus on
the Apocalypse and the Epistles of Paul. It forms, because of its
use (and abuse) in the Retreat which Stephen Dedalus makes in *A
Portrait*, the horrifying basis for Stephen's fear and detestation of
Catholicism. Father Arnall, whose drawn, pale face is lit by "a shaft
of wan light . . . filtered" between the last blind and the sash,
and whose lean figure is backed by "the battleworn mail armour of
angels" (*P* 116), preaches through most of the central chapter on
"Remember only thy last things." In stating his text, Father Arnall
cites Ecclesiastes instead of the correct Biblical source, Ecclesiasticus. The correct Biblical text, in the Douay version Arnall
would have used had he looked it up, is "remember thy last end."

That text, had Arnall stuck to its literal sense, would have limited him to one topic. But apparently Arnall did not look it up. It seems he derives his text from the Italian book on which Joyce modeled the Retreat, *Hell Opened to Christians*, by Giovanni Pietro Pinamonti, S.J., published in 1688. Arnall's version of the text is an acceptable translation of the Italian of Pinamonti, and the source given by Pinamonti is "Eccl. vii." As James Thrane points out in his excellent "Joyce's Sermon on Hell," *Joyce* would have had to look up the reference to get the verse number. Thrane perceptively speculates that if Joyce did, he probably was deliberate in putting the "free" text and the blunder of Ecclesiastes in Arnall's mouth.[5] I further suspect that Joyce, working from that "Eccl. vii," looked up Ecclesiastes first, since it comes first in the Douay Bible (in Protestant Bibles Ecclesiasticus is among the Apocrypha), and, not finding the text, went on through the Canticle of Canticles (central in *Chamber Music*) and Wisdom (important in Oxen of the Sun, where "wisdom hath built herself a house" [*U* 394] stresses the basic theme of feminine power in the book and in human experience) into Ecclesiasticus, where he found, in the Douay numbering, 7:40 to be the correct chapter and verse. But, as I speculate, having himself been mistaken in his first try, it then occurred to him that if Arnall had not looked it up, he might also not know which biblical book "Eccl." referred to. Thus a pleasant, easy way to question the infallibility of Jesuits fell in his lap. A trifling complication would then remain: how did Arnall get that tricky business of the correct verse number right?

But before my own Jesuit mind another possibility rises up, not likely (I must admit) to have occurred even to the endlessly ingenious mind of young Joyce. In Father Arnall's youth, neither the word "eschatology" nor the science it was coined to specify were as faddish and as central in theological interest as they were when Joyce wrote the Retreat for *A Portrait*. Hence Joyce's character might have lacked the aspects of theological interest and training which would have made the text especially significant. Young Joyce, then, might have slightly misimagined his character, saddling him with an "error" which would, more or less, have embarrassed a Jesuit educated in the milieu in which Joyce himself developed, but which could have been a comfortably understandable slip in an old Jesuit preaching in 1898. This situation suggests itself to my imagination, I am aware, only because I am thinking of the operation of "eschatology" (*FW* 482.33), but it stresses for me the possible operation of that word in the imagination of the young Joyce who brought the old Father Arnall into being.

What the mature Joyce did know was that "eschatology" had been constructed from learned Greek words in relatively recent times by persons less interested in words that in "science," as "transsubstantiation" had been constructed from Latin terms for similar theological purposes by Roman Aristotelean theologians about A.D. 1070. Joyce's marvelous literary use of the history-saturated "transmute" and "transsubstantiate" comes to a thundering climax in his ambivalent use of "transaccidentated" (*FW* 186.3−4). That last was coined, perhaps by Duns Scotus, merely to dismiss the possibility in the orthodox theory of transsubstantiation of a change of accidents. Later the word was wielded with power by Wycliffe and Luther and others who loathed the "scientific" distortions they seemed to perceive in "transubstantiation" (as the word is unfortunately and ineptly spelled in current convention). Joyce uses all its potentialities, as I have *ad nauseam* pointed out elsewhere.

Joyce liked to make such coinages himself, and did it with marvelous literary skill. "Astroglodynamonologos" (*FW* 194.16−17), for example, sounds forth Greek echoes of Theseus's

> The poet's eye, in a fine frenzy rolling,
> Doth glance from heaven to earth, from earth to heaven,
> And as imagination bodies forth
> The forms of things unknown. . . . (*Midsummer Night's Dream*,
>   V.i.12−15)

(That "unknown," by the way, has overtones unsuspected by the complacent Theseus, contemptuous as he is of suprarational mystery.) Joyce melds *astron*, *troglodutes*, *dunamis*, *mono*, *monolog*, *logos*, and *os* into a powerful, beautiful coinage to express his own new artistic dogmas, embodied in Shem. He provides on the same page, from the Hebrew *ba'alzebub*, a new Tetragrammaton for the principle of evil, appropriate in the context of Shaun's condemnation of Shem, "blzb" (*FW* 194.17).

Surely Joyce could look upon the Greek elements in "eschatology" with friendly interest, and could further be aware, as increasingly few of his readers are—so it would seem from much current criticism, distrustful as it is of the implications of human freedom and of traditional metaphysics—of the theological depths of the word's confrontation with infinity, a matter of basic importance both to the theologian and to the literary artist.

In my view, Joyce in the text under consideration is building specifically on Shakespeare's text in *A Midsummer Night's Dream.* Shakespeare's Bottom, when he attempts to express his "most rare vision," his ineffable experience of being embraced by a fairy queen, attempts to quote Paul's words: "The eye of man hath not heard, the eare of man hath not seen, mans hand is not able to taste, his tongue to conceive, nor his heart to report, what my dreame was" (*MND* IV.i.216–19). Paul had turned to Isaiah for words to express his own insight into the embrace of a human animal by the infinite Being: "But, as it is written, 'What no eye has seen, nor ear heard, nor the heart of man conceived, what God has prepared for those who love him'" (I Cor. 2:9). I hear Joyce echoing Shakespeare's use of Paul's text: "What can't be coded can be decorded if an ear aye sieze what no eye ere grieved for" (*FW* 482.34–36).

Shakespeare further realized well, as Paul did, that only the inspired prophet can by miracle ("unless this miracle have might,/ That in black ink my love may still shine bright," Sonnet 65) find the words and music to express the inexpressible. Therefore Bottom looks to Peter Quince, as Paul looked to Isaiah, as Shakespeare looked to Paul, as Joyce looked to Shakespeare. All realize the confrontation with infinity, the "dream" of the existence of love, which builds necessarily on the fact of the existence of human freedom of choice. Without freedom, love is impossible. Freedom generates the second element of eschatology, "judgment." And freedom, in its tension between "faith" and "fate," between the infinity of God's mastery and the quasi-infinite power of human choice, cannot be comprehended by human reason. Infinity, reached for by our apprehension, confounds our comprehension: "It shall be called Bottom's Dream, because it hath no bottom" (*MND* IV.i.220–21).

We cannot "code" the mystery of human experience, nor the depths of the human word. Words themselves we code conventionally and think, perhaps, that we have them tamed. Humpty Dumpty, who in his rational looking-glass world faintly foreglimmered the masterful Shaun, approached literary criticism with confidence:

> "When *I* use a word," Humpty Dumpty said, in rather a scornful tone, "it means just what I choose it to mean—neither more nor less."
>
> "The question is," said Alice, "whether you *can* make words mean so many different things."
>
> "The question is," said Humpty Dumpty, "which is to be master—that's all." [6]

Much more than Lewis Carroll does, Joyce probes the human word; Joyce knows that the "what" of "what can't be coded" is infinite mystery. It has no bottom. The brain is ultimately helpless. But the heart, the "cor," can hear in the music of the words the expression of Bottom's dream and (in Paul's as in Joyce's faith) intuit the joy that transcends death: "Death is swallowed up in victory. O death, where is thy victory? O death, where is thy sting?" (I Cor. 15:54–5). Thus, to make Peter's poem the more "gracious" (in Pauline vision, "grace" is divine life and love), Bottom will sing it in Peter's strange "comedy" at Thisby's death.

The "ear" does the seizing ("sieze" in Joyce's text I take as a "coding" of the necessity, in matters of faith, to transcend conventional rational rules, and perhaps to warn against Shaun's habit of putting the eye before the ear), and the "eye," which grieves over what can be seen, what is available to human senses and reason, will, left to itself, be left with its grief. Thus Margaret in Hopkins's "Spring and Fall" grieves over goldengrove unleaving, and must, as the speaker of the poem tells her, go deeper than the coding of mouth and mind, must reach the depths of the heart's "hearing," of faith's "guessing," of "decording" and reaching:

> Nor mouth had, no nor mind, expressed
> What heart heard of, ghost guessed. . . .[7]

"Aye" and "ere" demand attention. Both express time, but not from exactly the same angle. "Prouts," by the way, which one would expect to be singular as the name of Father Prout, the Cork priest and later brilliant newspaper correspondent, author of the time-keeping "Bells of Shandon" which sound here and there through *Finnegans Wake*. However, Prouts is plural for two reasons: Prout, in this Cork passage of Munster Mark, represents all poets; and secondly (I opine) he is also Proust, who did not keep time but attempted to bring it into the evanescent flow of the present. Joyce described Proust's achievement as "analytic still life."[8] Joyce was not much impressed, apparently, with Proust's efforts to master time. I understand Joyce's phrase to mean that analysis abstracts time from its real ever-changing flow and produces a merely mental still-life—that is, dead—reproduction. Depending on intuition reaching beyond analysis, Joyce aims at a living dynamic analogy.

In any case, "aye," confusedly mingled in our language with "ay," may be pronounced so as to rhyme with "hay" or with "eye." Both pronunciations have advantages here. The "hay" vowel, for which the *O.E.D.* prefers the spelling "ay," would, as the *O.E.D.* suggests, produce the meaning of "time," indefinite as to before and after, but open to the expression of future time, as in *Macbeth*'s "Let this pernitious houre/Stand aye accursed in the Kalender" (IV.i.134) or Mrs. Browning's "The love will last for aye."[9] The pronunciation "eye," for which the *O.E.D.* prefers the spelling "aye," is an affirmative response to a question. This latter pronunciation would more perfectly counterpoint with the following "eye" in the text of *Finnegans Wake*, but the time element seems to me the important one in meaning, so that I choose (usually) to pronounce it as a "hay" rhyme. The contrast of vowels still counterpoints, and the hesitation in one's imagination gives the effect of the other pronunciation anyway. The imagination of a *reader* does not, like the imagination of a *hearer*, depend solely on the ear. A reader must at times choose what kind of a hearer he or she will be.

Pronounced as rhyming with "hay," the word suggests to me a reason for the unconventional spelling of "sieze." The tag verse nuns taught me more than half a century ago was, I judge, identical or closely similar to one Joyce and perhaps Joyce's children learned: "*I before e except after c, or when sounded like a, as in neighbour and weigh.*" Since "seize" is one of numerous exceptions, one can pick up a code here (at least I do) that exceptions occur in all human certitudes based on or conditioned by convention (as most are, at least those linked with "fate"). This will then be true also for "aye" meaning "always." It may then be that we will settle for "aye" here as meaning this present moment in time, granting that in our constant change—"moving and changing every part of the time" (*FW* 118.22–23)—we can really isolate a passing moment. *Finnegans Wake* does not encourage easy certitudes.

"Ere," on the other hand, related as it is to "early," suggests past time. One of the things human eyes have most universally grieved for (or, as in German *greifen*, seized) is death. But universally too (at least broadly speaking), human ears have heard what human eyes have not seen, and have dug graves and treasured embalmed mummies and given other signs of survival for aye—a Bottom's Dream, because it hath no bottom.

The odd-nosed man and the extraordinarily beautiful woman (*FW* 403.7–12) have many identities, as is usual in that evershifting "mobiling so wobiling" evocation of more-than-Proustian shadowy "remembrandts." The one of special interest to me here is that of the actors in *Bottom's Dream*. The evidence of their presence is not overwhelming, but sufficient for me: the "Come not nere!" with which Titania's fairies charmed evils from her bower (*MND* II.ii.12 and *FW* 403.17); and Bottom's "as gently as any sucking dove" echoed in "in her dhove's suckling" (*MND* I.ii.84 and *FW* 403.16–17). With my mind conditioned by these echoes (prepared also by earlier ones and confirmed by later ones, especially the names given to this pair in a later setting), I find it possible to discern hints in many other words on the page, as, for example, the nose of a wild ass involved in "becco of wild hindigan" (*FW* 403.13).

I see also a profound underlying revelation of Joyce's own artistic realization of the dangers involved in his echoing of the artists who influenced him. The "translated" monster, whose name "Titubante" comes from Vergil (Peter Quince happily cries, "Bless thee, Bottom! Bless thee! Thou art translated"—*MND* III.i.121), seems to be unlike the family of Ovid, a Latin who wrote about Greeks, "nought like the nasoes" (*FW* 403.7). Publius Ovidius Naso, a man of large nose, was an important figure in Joyce's as in Stephen's development. He was the artificer who created the "old artificer" to whom Stephen prayed and whose name he bore; he created the minotaur and maze imagery for Stephen; he gave the model of the careful workman who must construct words in new ways, "unknown arts," in order to avoid being dominated and crushed by great predecessors. Ovid sought "unknown arts" to circumvent the overwhelming influence of Vergil, as Joyce had to avoid being smothered by Sophocles, knocked out by Shakespeare, made a zero (a "naught") by Dante, bastardized by Moses—"Suffoclose! Shikespower! Seudodanto! Anonymoses!" (*FW* 47.19)—even out-rhymed by Yeats. Especially (as *FW* 403 may suggest) Joyce had to avoid slavish imitation of Ovid himself, that devious master of invention, so that he too could be "nought like the nasoes."

The names of the loving pair show up in a stage scene (*FW* 501) similar to (perhaps identical with, except for the verbal expression of it) the boxed ("capsules") stage (*FW* 403; the set is described with almost daylight clarity on *FW* 558–59). The bower, clearer because dawn is approaching and perhaps because we have added an anagogical level or two, takes on, under a flood of Christmas hymns, tones of the Cave of Bethlehem, where the Word-made-flesh came into the world "on a particular lukesummer night" (*FW* 501.16). The pair is named: "From Miss Somer's nice dream back to Mad

Winthrop's delugium stramens" (*FW* 502.29–30). "We are such stuff as dreams are made on" and Somer's shipwreck may be echoed from *The Tempest*, and *The Winter's Tale* has mad aspects, but I see both names basically as treatments of *A Midsummer Night's Dream*. Bottom, whose ass's thropple (throat) will match his "self-tinted, wrinkling, ruddled" nose (*FW* 403.7–8, perhaps reflecting Arthur Rackham's dramatic painting of the singing Bottom), had turned the summer night into a mad fall or winter hunting scene for his confreres, frightening them into flight like wild geese that "madly sweep the sky" (*MND* III.ii.32). Bottom's throat, too, had been unable to produce words to express his incredible dream. To those who observed his state, it must indeed have seemed a "delirium tremens." But to him, as Titania caressed his long ears and offered him new nuts, it seemed indeed a "delugium stramens." "Stramens" is Latin for straw, and Bottom prefers "good hay" to all other food (*MND* IV.i.35).

Thus for me *Bottom's Dream* shines with something of that flood of light that blinded Paul on his quest to Damascus, where eye ceased to function and ear received the Word. Something of that light and that music rises for me in the counterpointed words of *Finnegans Wake*. Anybody can, I believe, if that somebody loves words and is willing to listen with open and cheerful ears, hear in the words of *Finnegans Wake* an expression of the slow unfolding of "all marry-voising moodmoulded cyclewheeling history" (*FW* 186.1–2), including each one's own. Like the great dreamers of the human race, we may in some fashion be filled with light on our own road to Damascus. Young Joyce set out to "try myself," and somehow his ears seized what his eyes alone could not see. Maybe if we too just listen, we may find like the brave crusading young Joyce "the faith in the soul, which changes all things and fills their inconstancy with light":

He is cured by faith who is sick of fate. The prouts who will invent a writing there ultimately is the poeta, still more learned, who discovered the raiding there originally. That's the point of eschatology our book of

kills reaches for now in soandso many counterpoint words. What can't be
coded can be decorded if an ear aye sieze what no eye ere grieved for. (*FW*
482.30–36)

Notes

1. A[lexander] L. R[inger], "Musical Composition," *New Encyclopaedia Britannica: Macropaedia*, 15th ed. (1974), XII, 717.

2. Joseph Otten, "Palestrina," *Catholic Encyclopedia* (1911), XI, 422.

3. Otten, p. 423.

4. Frank Budgen, *James Joyce and the Making of* Ulysses *and Other Writings*, intro. Clive Hart (London, etc.: Oxford Univ. Pr., 1972), p. 187.

5. James Thrane, "Joyce's Sermon on Hell," in *A James Joyce Miscellany*, Third Series, ed. Marvin Magalaner (Carbondale: Southern Illinois Univ. Pr., 1962), p. 75.

6. Lewis Carroll, *Through the Looking-Glass*, in *The Annotated Alice*, ed. Martin Gardner (New York: Bramhall House, 1960), p. 269.

7. Gerard Manley Hopkins, *Poems*, ed. W. H. Gardner and N. H. MacKenzie, 4th ed. (London, etc.: Oxford Univ. Pr., 1967), p. 89.

8. Richard Ellmann, *James Joyce* (New York: Oxford Univ. Pr., 1959), p. 524.

9. Elizabeth Barrett Browning, "A Romance of the Ganges," *Complete Poetical Works*, ed. Harriet Waters Preston (Boston: Houghton Mifflin, 1900), p. 31.

Contributors
Index

Contributors

Morris Beja is a Professor of English at Ohio State University, where he teaches modern literature and film. He is the author of *Epiphany in the Modern Novel* and *Film and Literature*, and the editor of *Psychological Fiction* and of volumes of critical essays on Joyce's *Dubliners* and *A Portrait*, Virginia Woolf's *To the Lighthouse*, and (forthcoming) Samuel Beckett. He edits the *James Joyce Foundation Newsletter* and presently serves as Foundation president.

Shari Benstock and Bernard Benstock are joining the faculty of the University of Tulsa as Senior Fellow in the Faculty of Modern Letters and as chairman of the Department of Foreign Languages and Comparative Literature. Their most recent book is *Who's He When He's at Home: A James Joyce Directory* (University of Illinois Press). Shari Benstock has published articles on Joyce in *Style, Contemporary Literature, Modern Fiction Studies, Centennial Review*, and *James Joyce Quarterly*; forthcoming publications include *ELH* and the *Journal of Narrative Technique* (co-author with Bernard Benstock). Bernard Benstock has recently edited *Pomes for James Joyce* (Malton Press), *The Seventh of Joyce* (Indiana University Press), a special Joyce issue of *Comparative Literature Studies*, and co-edited *James Joyce: An International Perspective* with S. H. Bushrui.

Robert Boyle, S.J., began his college career under Robert Faner at S.I.N.U. in Carbondale in 1933 and concluded it under Cleanth Brooks at Yale in 1955. At Regis College in Denver he introduced Thomas Staley to Joyce, published *Metaphor in Hopkins* in 1961, provided the first article for the *James Joyce Quarterly*, shifted to Marquette University in Milwaukee in 1968, published *James Joyce's Pauline Vision* (the proper title of which is *Man Is but an Ass*) in 1978, and is at present (February 1982) Distinguished Visiting Professor at the University of Delaware.

Sheldon Brivic, Associate Professor of English at Temple University, is the author of *Joyce Between Freud and Jung*. His most recent article, "Joyce and the Metaphysics of Creation," appeared in the *Crane Bag*, an Irish review. He is completing a book on how Joyce manifests himself as a presence in his work, the tentative title of which is *The Minds of Joyce*.

Margaret Church was Professor of English and Comparative Literature at Purdue University, edited *Modern Fiction Studies* and chaired Comparative Literature. She was author of *Time and Reality: Studies in Contemporary Fiction* (1963), which includes a chapter on Joyce; of *Don Quixote, Knight of La Mancha* (1971); and of many articles on modern fiction, among them ten on Joyce. Her new book *Structure and Theme:* Don Quixote *to James Joyce* will be published by the Ohio State University Press in March 1983. She was a trustee of the James Joyce Foundation. In 1942, she worked for her M.A. at Columbia University under the direction of William York Tindall.

Alan M. Cohn is Humanities Librarian and Professor of English, Southern Illinois University at Carbondale. He is bibliographer for the *James Joyce Quarterly*, co-bibliographer for the *Dickens Studies Newsletter*, and co-editor of *ICarbS* and *The Cumulated Dickens Checklist, 1970–1979*. His work has also appeared in *PMLA*, *Publications of the Bibliographical Society of America*, and elsewhere.

Edmund L. Epstein is Professor of English at Queens College—CUNY and at the CUNY Graduate Center. He edited the *James Joyce Review* and is on the Board of Advisors of the *James Joyce Quarterly*. He is at present the editor of *Language and Style*. He is the author of *The Ordeal of Stephen Dedalus*, and editor of *A Starchamber*

Quiry: A Joyce Centennial Publication—1882–1982. He has also published widely on modern literature and linguistics.

Suzette A. Henke is Associate Professor of English at the State University of New York at Binghamton. She is author of *Joyce's Moraculous Sindbook: A Study of* Ulysses (Ohio State University Press, 1978) and co-editor, with Elaine Unkeless, of *Women in Joyce* (University of Illinois Press, 1982), a collection of essays on Joyce's female characters. Professor Henke has published articles and reviews on modern literature in such journals as the *James Joyce Quarterly*, the *Virginia Woolf Quarterly*, the *Journal of Aesthetics and Art Criticism*, the *American Imago*, *Modern British Literature*, the *Canadian Journal of Irish Studies*, *Modern Fiction Studies*, and the *Beckett Circle*.

Patrick A. McCarthy is Associate Professor of English at the University of Miami in Coral Gables, Florida, where he teaches a variety of courses in twentieth century literature. In addition to numerous articles on Joyce and other modern writers he has published two books: *The Riddles of* Finnegans Wake (1980) and *Olaf Stapledon* (1982). At present he is working on a book that will examine the reader's situation in *Ulysses* and *Finnegans Wake*.

Richard F. Peterson is Professor of English at Southern Illinois University at Carbondale. He is the author of *Mary Lavin* (1978) and *William Butler Yeats* (1982). His writings on Irish literature have appeared in *Modern Fiction Studies*, *Studies in Short Fiction*, *Éire-Ireland*, the *Journal of Irish Literature*, the *James Joyce Quarterly* and *The Sean O'Casey Review*. Essays are scheduled for publication in the *Irish Renaissance Annual* and the *Yeats Annual*.

Fritz Senn took an amateur interest in Joyce long ago and has become an occasional Visiting Professor in the States. He is connected with the *James Joyce Quarterly*, *A Wake Newslitter*, and the James Joyce Foundation, and has been one of the initiators of the James Joyce Symposia. He has written widely on Joyce in various books and journals.

Index

Work in Progress

Designed by David Ford

Set in Linotron Garamond No. 3
by G & S Typesetters, Inc.

Printed by Vail-Ballou Press
on Vail-Ballou's Antique Cream

Bound by Vail-Ballou Press
in Joanna Arrestox linen
and stamped in silver
with Multicolor Antique Donegal endsheets